STUDIES ON INDUSTRIAL PRODUCTIVITY:
SELECTED WORKS

Volume 4

STRATEGIC INVESTMENT PLANNING WITH TECHNOLOGY CHOICE IN MANUFACTURING SYSTEMS

STRATEGIC INVESTMENT PLANNING WITH TECHNOLOGY CHOICE IN MANUFACTURING SYSTEMS

SHAN LING LI

LONDON AND NEW YORK

First published in 1994 by Garland Publishing Inc.

This edition first published in 2019
by Routledge
2 Park Square, Milton Park, Abingdon, Oxon OX14 4RN

and by Routledge
711 Third Avenue, New York, NY 10017

Routledge is an imprint of the Taylor & Francis Group, an informa business

© 1994 Shan Ling Li

British Library Cataloguing in Publication Data
A catalogue record for this book is available from the British Library

ISBN: 978-1-138-61548-9 (Set)
ISBN: 978-0-429-44077-9 (Set) (ebk)
ISBN: 978-1-138-32438-1 (Volume 4) (hbk)
ISBN: 978-0-429-45090-7 (Volume 4) (ebk)

Publisher's Note
The publisher has gone to great lengths to ensure the quality of this reprint but points out that some imperfections in the original copies may be apparent.

Disclaimer
The publisher has made every effort to trace copyright holders and would welcome correspondence from those they have been unable to trace.

STRATEGIC INVESTMENT PLANNING WITH TECHNOLOGY CHOICE IN MANUFACTURING SYSTEMS

SHAN LING LI

GARLAND PUBLISHING, Inc.
NEW YORK & LONDON / 1994

Library of Congress Cataloging-in-Publication Data

Li, Shan Ling, 1949–
    Strategic investment planning with technology choice in manufacturing systems / Shan Ling Li.
        p.   cm. — (Garland studies on industrial productivity)
    Based on the author's thesis (Ph.D.—University of Texas at Austin).
    Includes bibliographical references (p.   ) and index.
    ISBN 0–8153–1594–5 (alk. paper)
    1. Manufactures—Capital investments—Planning. 2. Manufacturing processes—Decision making. 3. Manufacturing resource planning.
I. Title. II. Series.
HD9720.5.L5   1994
670'.68'4—dc20   93–38434
                                                      CIP

Printed on acid-free, 250-year-life paper
Manufactured in the United States of America

Dedicated to

My Parents

CONTENTS

List of Tables   **xi**
List of Figures   **xiii**
Preface   **xv**
Acknowledgments   **xvii**

Chapter 1 Introduction   **3**
1.1 Introduction   3
1.2 Contribution   4
1.3 Organization of the Study   5

Chapter 2 An Overview: Technology Selection and Capacity Planning for Manufacturing Systems   **7**
2.1 Characteristics of the Technology Selection and Capacity Expansion Problem   8
2.2 Justification Approaches for Technology Selection   13
    2.2.1 Practical Approaches   13
    2.2.2 Modeling Approaches with Single Product   14
        2.2.2.1 Multi-Region Models   18
        2.2.2.2 Models with Technology Improvement   20
        2.2.2.3 Models with Stochastic Demand   22
    2.2.3 Modeling Approaches with Two Products   25
        2.2.3.1 Models with Deterministic Demand   26
        2.2.3.2 Models with Stochastic Demand   28
    2.2.4 Modeling Approaches with Multi-Products   31
        2.2.4.1 Models with Deterministic Demand   31
        2.2.4.2 Models with Stochastic Demand   33
2.3 Application in Technology Selection and Capacity Expansion   34
2.4 Conclusion   37

Chapter 3 Technology Choice and Capacity Expansion with Two Product Families: Tradeoffs Between Scale and Scope   **39**
3.1 Literature Review   41
3.2 Capacity Planning Problem   42
3.3 Initial Solution Procedure   46
    3.3.1 SMCP Approach   46
    3.3.2 SP Approach   47
3.4 Improvement Heuristics and Lower Bound   50

3.4.1 Improvement Heuristics   50
3.4.2 Lower Bound   52

3.5 Computational Results   53
3.6 Summary and Extension   57

**Chapter 4   Dynamic Capacity Expansion Problem with
Multiple Products: Technology Selection and Timing of
Capacity Additions**   **59**
4.1 Related Literature   61
4.2 The Capacity Expansion Problem (CP)   63
    4.2.1 Heuristics for CP (Phase 1)   65
    4.2.2 Improvement Heuristics (Phase 2)   68
4.3 Lower Bound and Optimal Solution to CP   69
    4.3.1 Aggregate Lower Bound   69
    4.3.2 Dual Lower Bound   70
    4.3.3 An Integer Programming Formulation
          of CP (ICP)   72
4.4 Computational Results   73
    4.4.1 Discussion of Results   74
    4.4.2 Related Comments   75
4.5 Conclusion   76

**Chapter 5   Technology Choice with Stochastic Demands
and Dynamic Capacity Allocation: A Two-Product
Analysis**   **79**
5.1 Problem Motivation and Related Research   81
5.2 An Investment Model for Technology Choice Problems with
    Two-Product Families   84
5.3 Analysis of TPCT(X_0), A Subproblem Related to TPCT   86
5.4 A Solution Procedure For TPCT   96
5.5 Conclusion Results   98
5.6 Conclusions   100

Chapter 5   Conclusion   **103**
6.1 Summary   103
6.2 Future Research   103

Tables   **105**

Figures   **111**

Appendixes   **123**
Appendix A   123
Appendix B   125
Appendix C   126
Appendix D   128
Appendix E   132
Appendix F   133
Appendix G   135
Appendix H   137

Bibliography   **139**
Index   **149**

LIST OF TABLES

Table 3.5   Summary of Computational Results   105

Table 4.4.1 Design of Computational Experiments   106

Table 4.4.1a Summary Results of Experiment with
             Power Cost Functions (small-sized,
             3 products, 5 periods)   107
Table 4.4.1b Summary Results of Experiment with
             Fixed Charge Cost Functions
             (3 products, 5 periods)   107

Table 4.4.1c Summary Results of Experiment with
             Power cost Functions (3 products, 5
             periods)   108

Table 4.4.1d Summary Results of Experiment with
             Power Cost Functions (5 products, 10
             periods)   108

Table 4.4.1e Summary Results of Experiment with
             Fixed Charge Cost Functions
             (5 products, 10 periods)   108

Table 5.5.1 Data for the Computational Study   109

Table 5.5.2 Computational Results for Linear and Fixed
             Charge Cost Functions   110

Table 5.5.3 Computational Results for Power Cost Functions 110

LIST OF FIGURES

Figure 2.1a: Multi-Dimensioned Attributes of Demand   111

Figure 2.1b: Some Sample Demand Patterns   112

Figure 2.2.2: Process of Demand Growth and Capacity
                Expansion   113

Figure 2.2.3.1 A Network-Flow Representation for Problem LS   114

Figure 3.3.1   The Alternative Expansion Strategies   115

Figure 3.4.1   Improvement Heuristic Procedures   116

Figure 4.2.1   Initial Solution for CP (Phase I)   117

Figure 4.2.2   Improvement Heuristic Procedures (Phase II)   118

Figure 4.3.2   The Lower Bound of CP   119

Figure 5.3.1   Feasible Region for Model TPCT   120

Figure 5.3.2   Feasible Regions for $T(X_0)$ 121

Figure 5.3.3   Flow Chart of the Search Procedure for $T(X_0)$ 122

LIST OF FIGURES

PREFACE

In this study, I examine problems related to investment planning, capacity additions, and choice of technology in dynamic manufacturing systems characterized by multiple products, dynamic demand growth, uncertainty in demand, and availability of alternative technologies. The motivation for this research comes from recent developments in the field of flexible technology such as CAM and CIM. There is a growing interest to invest in these perhaps more expensive technologies in order to provide a competitive edge in such forms as rapid responses to changing customer requirements, flexibility in product mix, short product life cycles, etc. The objective of this study is to develop a model-based methodology that focuses on tradeoffs between flexible and conventional technology. The research in this dissertation is directed to the development of tools to support investment decisions in production capacity over medium- and long-term planning horizons.

I first examine a two-product dynamic investment model for making technology choices and expansion decisions over a finite planning horizon. Discrete period, finite horizon mathematical programs are used to determine the optimal mix of dedicated and flexible technologies. Since these problems are difficult to solve optimally, a two-phase heuristic procedure is developed to obtain good expansion schedules.

Next, the two-product model is extended to multiple products. These extensions result in subproblems that are hard to solve, and hence I focus on the development of approximations and lower bounds. The computational experiments show that the heuristics and lower bound approaches work very well. Investment strategies are also derived from the extensive computational experiments.

Finally, I expand the scope of the models to incorporate issues related to uncertainty and examine the role of flexible technology and its benefits. Service level, one of the important measures of service, is incorporated in our problem. I provide two stochastic investment models to determine optimal mix of technologies and minimum total investment cost.

ACKNOWLEDGMENTS

This book grew out of my dissertation at University of Texas at Austin and I am grateful to my advisor, Dr. Devanath Tirupati for his knowledge, guidance and support. I would like to thank Dr. William W. Cooper for his insightful comments on my research and for his continuing encouragement.

I would also like to thank Dr. James A. Fitzsimmons, Dr. Hirofumi Mastuo and Dr. Robert S. Sullivan. Their valuable comments and suggestions for dissertation are substantial. I owe a special debt to Mr. Stephen Ahern and Ms. Laila Lampsa who spent tremendous time in editing this book.

In addition, I wish to acknowledge the financial support under NFS Grant DDM-8957-189 and NSERC Grant 22773.

My editors, Dr. Stuart Bruchey and Mr. Robert McKenzie have been spirited and dedicated champions; they believed in this book from the beginning and contributed to it in continuous encouragement.

Finally, I would like to thank my parents for all they have done to make this book possible. I take great joy in dedicating this book to my parents.

Strategic Investment Planning with Technology Choice in Manufacturing Systems

I. INTRODUCTION

1.1 INTRODUCTION

The annual increase in productivity of the United States in the past ten years is the lowest among all industrial nations, including Japan, West Germany, France, Italy, and England (Krajewski and Ritzman 1987). The acquisition of flexible manufacturing technology has been suggested as one solution to reverse this trend. Kantrow (1980) and Gerwin (1989) argue that flexible technology is an essential element to increase a firm's long-term competitive position. Today many firms have placed huge bets on new flexible technologies.

Many advantages can be enumerated to support the acquisition of flexible manufacturing technology: quick response to the change in market demand, lead time reduction, increased demand due to increased product flexibility, and improved quality of goods and services produced. For example, recent developments in modern technologies such as CAM, CAD, CIM and FMS provide operational flexibility and permit production of a variety of products with little or no change over costs. However, the flexibility that modern technologies can provide is at the expense of the increased cost of acquiring flexible manufacturing capacity, as compared to dedicated technologies with specialized equipment that is designed to produce a limited range of products more efficiently.

However, many firms are finding that their available tools for evaluating investments in flexible technology often contradict the intuition of their managers. Many of them perceive significant benefits from acquiring flexible manufacturing systems (FMS and CIM). Kaplan (1986) acknowledges that even a very careful application of discounted cash flow techniques commonly used to evaluate a potential investment in flexible technology will not capture the strategic benefits of flexibility. Kaplan suggests that managerial judgement be applied to decide whether the strategic benefits of an investment in flexible technology outweigh the difference, or gap, between the investment cost and the quantifiable benefits.

1.2 CONTRIBUTION

In this study, my objective is to model some of the key characteristics of modern technologies in order to describe the economic tradeoffs between acquisition of flexible capacity and the firm's ability to respond to dynamic, uncertain demands. Since incorporation of features such as scale and scope economies results in nonlinear programs that are hard to solve optimally, I focus on the development of approximation and heuristic approaches.

One of the main contributions of this study is to provide an integration of issues in capacity planning and technology choice. In fact, decisions on appropriate mixes of dedicated and flexible capacity involve many complex considerations such as economies of scale, likely demand patterns, mix flexibility, service level, etc. The models developed in this study are able to capture these important characteristics and to result in managerially meaningful solutions.

Second, I also develop approximations, heuristics, and lower bounds to solve the models for which it is difficult to obtain optimal solutions. The solution procedures are based on easily solvable sequences of subproblems derived from the planning problems. The heuristics require modest computational effort and my results demonstrate that these procedures can be used to obtain a good understanding of the tradeoffs involved in making technology and capacity additions.

Finally, I illustrate the scope of my models and computational procedures by deriving investment strategies and the optimal mix of technologies for some typical scenarios. These results suggest that investments in flexible technology should be made early in the planning horizon, and that flexible technology can play the role of capacity cushion in meeting dynamic (deterministic) demands. I also examine the conditions necessary for a firm to make technology and investment choices to achieve pre-specified service levels.

Finally, I explore the sensitivity of a firm's optimal capacity investment decision to key components--namely, to demand patterns, to the cost of flexible and dedicated technology, to economies of scale in investment of technologies, to the underlying distribution of product demand, and to the the pre-specified service levels of products.

1.3 ORGANIZATION OF THE STUDY

This study is organized as follows: Chapter 2 reviews literature that addresses issues related to capacity additions over long-term horizons and dynamic growth in demand in the area of investment planning. Chapter 3 examines a two-product dynamic investment model for making technology choices and expansion decisions over a finite planning horizon. Chapter 4 extends the model in Chapter 3 to a multiple-product case. Due to the complexity of the extended model, solution procedures and lower bounds are developed. Chapter 5 incorporates issues related to uncertainty and examines the role of flexible technology and its benefits in a stochastic environment. Chapter 6 contains conclusions and explores opportunities for further research.

II. AN OVERVIEW: TECHNOLOGY SELECTION AND CAPACITY PLANNING FOR MANUFACTURING SYSTEMS

Capacity expansion decisions in most industries usually involve substantial capital investments and have received considerable attention from both academicians and practitioners. These decisions typically require an understanding of the tradeoffs between several related factors and cannot be made in isolation. For example, process and manufacturing technologies in chemical, electric power, fertilizer, engineering and communication industries are highly capital intensive and exhibit substantial scale economies. The availability of alternative technologies suggests that these choices between alternative technologies should be made together with the expansion decisions. For firms facing demands distributed over geographical regions, plant location and expansion decisions are linked and there is also a tradeoff between investment and transportation costs. The reader may note that any combination of these factors together with the dynamics of product demand make technology choice and expansion decisions extremely complex.

In most process industries, automation and integration have been continuing trends for decades and the methodologies and models for supporting capacity and technology decisions must accommodate their more important characteristics. However, in discrete goods manufacturing, recent developments in modern technologies such as flexible manufacturing systems (FMS), computer integrated manufacturing (CIM), computer aided design (CAD), and flexible automation (FA) permit production of a wide variety of products with small changeover costs. Increased competition in the marketplace, particularly from overseas manufacturers, has resulted in short product cycles and has put a premium on flexibility in changing product mix. Together, these factors encourage investments in facilities capable of producing several product families. The presence of economies of scale

7

introduces additional complexity, thus making expansion decisions even more intricate.

My objective in this chapter is to provide the reader with an overview of the methodologies that are available for supporting technology and capacity decisions. This chapter is directed toward practitioners with modeling interests, and researchers with an application focus. The goal is to provide the reader with a flavor of the research in the area and to describe its role in making technology choices and expansion decisions. Thus I concentrate on modeling issues and applications rather than on theoretical results. (For a comprehensive review of the literature focusing on the economic aspects of evaluation of flexible technologies, I refer the reader to a recent survey by Fine and Freund (1990).) Since the resulting decision problems are complex and difficult to solve for exact optima, I elaborate on heuristic procedures and approximation methods that have been developed in this context.

This chapter is organized as follows: in the following section, Section 2.1, I describe the major factors that play a key role in technology and capacity choices. Section 2.2 is devoted to models and methodologies that have been developed to support these strategic and tactical decisions. Several applications of these methods are discussed in Section 2.3. Finally, I conclude in Section 2.4 with a summary of outstanding issues.

2.1 CHARACTERISTICS OF THE TECHNOLOGY SELECTION AND CAPACITY EXPANSION PROBLEM

As indicated in the introduction, a number of factors influence strategic choices related to the technology selection and capacity additions. These include, among others, product mix characteristics, technology alternatives, cost parameters, length of the planning horizon, etc. In this section, I briefly describe the key factors of the capacity planning problem.

Product Mix
The range of products manufactured by a plant is a function of the production technology used and, to a large degree, determines the complexity of the planning problem. The simplest case is represented by a firm producing a single homogeneous product. Electricity generation in the power industry is a classic example that fits this case. The single product model can also be used for firms producing several variants of a basic product line. A stable product mix in such cases will

permit aggregation of all variants into a single product. Several examples in the chemical and process industry fit such a model fairly well. In contrast to the fairly homogeneous products in the foregoing examples, the product mix in discrete part manufacturing is quite diverse and dynamic. Between these extremes, a wide range of product mix patterns can be found. For example, in the oil refining industry the product mix is determined primarily by the choice of inputs and by the processing technology. Similarly, in the fertilizer industry, the product mix may consist of substitutable products (for example, coal- and oil-based fertilizers) that are produced from entirely different set of inputs and production processes. In such cases, the planning problem may be modeled as a single product case with alternate technologies.

Product mix plays an important role in technology selection because many factors related to product mix may complicate these decisions. In the case of a single product, the technology choice decision focuses merely on the cost structure of different technologies since all of them have a specific function associated with producing a single product (see Cohen and Halperin (1986)). When a firm produces multiple products, many factors are involved in the decisions, such as operational flexibility (whether it is dedicated, semi-flexible or flexible), and the cost of alternative technologies. Evaluation of the tradeoffs between functions and costs of technologies becomes extremely difficult with a large number of products and a dynamic product mix.

Demand

Technology and capacity decisions are driven by product demands that may be characterized along several dimensions. This multidimensional attribute is perhaps the single most important factor that determines the investment levels and the amount of capacity additions. In most planning problems product demands are assumed to be given (perhaps based on market analysis) and the objective is to develop medium- or long-term plans to meet this demand. However, in some integrative approaches, the demand levels are treated as decision variables to be determined in conjunction with choices related to production facilities. Since the former case is more common, in this chapter I focus mostly on models and methods in which demand is considered to be an exogenous parameter.

Figure 2.1a portrays various factors that determine product demand characteristics. In what follows, I briefly elaborate on some of these aspects. One of the key features that determines the complexity of the planning problem relates to modeling of demand as either a stochastic or a deterministic process. Clearly, actual demand is almost always uncertain and is stochastic. However, deterministic models are often easier to analyze and may be adequate for planning purposes. For example, for mature products with not very substantial random fluctuations in demand, it may be sufficient to make planning decisions based on average demands. Changes in demand can be met by intermediate term production planning with inventories and short term capacity changes. This kind of deterministic approach has an additional advantage in that data requirements are consistent with the information that is normally available as collected by firms and used by the decision hierarchy. Nevertheless, I can observe that while deterministic models are suitable for many applications, they do not capture some of the key flexibility benefits provided by modern integrative technologies such as CIM and FMS. In such situations, it is desirable to model the effect of uncertainties in demand and the role of flexibility explicitly. (This aspect is discussed in detail in Section 2.2.)

A second aspect that influences capacity decisions is the behavior of demand over time. In the simplest case, demand is time invariant and one-time decisions are sufficient (with provision for depreciation and loss of capacity). However, demands are often dynamic and changing patterns of demand become a key factor. Figure 2.1b describes several patterns that are commonly encountered in practice. Clearly, well-established growth patterns such as linear or geometric growth are easier to analyze. However, responsiveness to markets may give rise to general demand patterns as outlined in Figure 2.1b.

In environments with multiple products, the situation is further complicated by inter-product influences on demand. In the simplest case, the demands for different products may be considered independent, with production technology as the common factor. However, it is more common for facilities to manufacture products with either positively or negatively correlated demands. The former case can be observed in firms producing automobile components for the same type of car. For example, production of many correlate positively with production of body shells. Negatively correlated demands can be found in consumer electronics industry which produces a variety of substitutable products such as TV and radio sets.

Technology Choice

Traditionally, large volume mass production and low unit costs have been prime motivators in the development of manufacturing technologies. These objectives have been associated with dedicated technologies in the form of specialized equipment designed to produce a limited range of products in an efficient manner. Automobile assembly lines are classic examples of such production systems. However, in recent years there has been a growing trend toward the development of integrated technologies that provide great deal of operational flexibility. Automation and computer-controlled equipment to facilitate switch over between a variety of products are examples of such technologies. Other benefits of these modern technologies may include quality improvement and cost reduction, as when, for instance, numerous lengthy and costly set-up times are avoided.

As noted in the introduction, the development of integrative technologies has been a continuing phenomenon in process industries for several years, and the methodologies for their evaluation need to incorporate all relevant features. However, these developments are fairly recent and their features have not been fully captured in presently available evaluation models. This is a major weakness of the methodologies that are currently available for supporting capacity and technology decisions.

I note that between the two extremes of dedicated and flexible technologies, a wide range of production processes are available. For example, it is quite common to find technologies with limited flexibility that are capable of producing a subset of products. Another variant of flexible technology consists of essentially dedicated plants that are amenable for conversion from one type of product to another. Such conversions typically involve one-time investment costs and, in some cases, may be irreversible. Examples of convertible technologies can be found in the communications industry (cable production) and in the energy sector (furnaces capable of conversion from coal to oil and vice versa).

In summary, it is important to understand and model the key features of technology alternatives as they relate to capacity and equipment choices. This modeling aspect requires considerable knowledge and judgement and is important since it determines the relevance of the results provided by the model.

Cost Function

Clearly, cost is one of the important factors in technology selection. Linear functions are most popular and continue to be used over a wide range of applications. The primary motivation for their use is ease of analysis, and they may be appropriate in cases with no significant scale economies. However, it is well known that in several industries, investments in plant and equipment exhibit substantial scale economies (see, for example, Manne (1967) and Luss (1982)).

Concave functions that permit modeling of several types of scale economies have been used extensively in the development of analytical models for capacity planning. In practice, the two specific forms described below have been very useful in capturing cost characteristics exhibited by several production technologies.

(i)   Power function:

$f(x) = Kx^\alpha$ where $f(\cdot) = $ cost function
x = amount of capacity addition, $x \geq 0$
K = constant
α = economies of scale parameter, $0 < \alpha \leq 1$.

The power function has been found to be appropriate for process industries with significant scale economies such as chemicals, oil refining, fertilizers, cement, etc. A low value of α indicates large economies of scale and vice versa. For example, Manne (1967) suggests a value of α between 0.6 and 0.8 for such cases.

(ii)   Fixed-charge cost function:

$$f(x) = \begin{cases} 0 & \text{if } x = 0 \\ F+vx & \text{if } x > 0 \end{cases}$$

where F and v respectively are the fixed and variable costs in investment.

This form is particularly suitable for engineering and fabrication industries where capacity may be added in relatively small increments. It is also useful for incorporating administrative, financial and other expenses that are independent of the amount of capacity addition.

It should be mentioned that it is not necessary for these cost functions to be stationary over the planning horizon. This is an interesting and important feature to consider in some industries since technological advances could lead to cost reductions in the future.

Planning Horizon

In the short run, technology and equipment are fixed, and capacity planning relates to work force planning and decisions such as overtime operation, subcontracting part of the demand and smoothing production with inventory buildup. In contrast, technology and equipment choices are long-term decisions with the length of the planning horizon depending on many factors, including maturity of technology, level of investment and uncertainties in demands, costs, and dynamics of product mix.

Thus, for environments with a stable, mature product mix and well-defined, capital-intensive technology choices, long planning horizons are appropriate. For a rough-cut analysis in such cases, continuous-time, infinite-horizon models provide quick solutions with little computational effort (details are described in Section 2.2). With more dynamic demands and several choices in capacity and technology, discrete time and finite horizon models that explicitly consider the alternatives are required to describe the relevant tradeoffs. Typically, these problems are harder to solve and require specialized algorithms.

2.2 JUSTIFICATION APPROACHES FOR TECHNOLOGY SELECTION

In discrete parts manufacturing industries, recent developments in integrative technologies such as CIM and FMS have made it possible to design plants with planning horizons longer than individual product lifes. This can be particularly attractive since current trends suggest shortening product life in the market. As a result, manufacturing capabilities have become more important in defining the strategic position of a firm. A number of empirical studies indicate that while most managers have a good conceptual understanding of the benefits of modern technologies, methods for their evaluation and adoption are rather inadequate.

In this section I describe approaches for the evaluation of alternative technologies, and for the adoption of investment and capacity plans. I focus on the role of analytic models in supporting these high-level managerial decisions. Accordingly, Section 2.2.1 begins with a brief description of methods commonly employed in practice, and point out major weaknesses in capturing key tradeoffs. The remainder of the section is devoted to a description of optimization models and solution approaches. Section 2.2.2 focuses on models for the single product case while Sections 2.2.3 and 2.2.4, respectively, describe models for two- and multiple-product families.

2.2.1 PRACTICAL APPROACHES

Discounted cash flow methods such as net present value (NPV) and internal rate of return (IRR) are still some of the most popular methods employed in practice for project selection and capacity planning. While these methods have been successfully used in ranking projects and in developing capital budgets, it is important to recognize that these approaches provide only marginal cash flow analyses. This kind of marginal analysis focuses only on the values of incremental cash flows, and does not reflect many benefits incorporated in advanced technologies where flexibility may be an important consideration. For example,

Flexible Manufacturing Systems may have the benefits of reducing set-up times, increasing production efficiency, and improving manufacturing flexibility, which, to some extent, may be reflected in cash flow. Some of the benefits of flexible manufacturing such as quick response time to changing demands cannot be measured adequately by such cash flows, and hence there is a need for more comprehensive methods that take into account all relevant factors. In fact, much has been written recently on the difficulties of measuring manufacturing performance with traditional cost accounting methods (see Kaplan (1983); Cooper and Kaplan (1988a, 1988b); and Berliner and Brimson (1988)). In fact many firms have made their investments with either inadequate, or no, justification, and in fact, Kaplan (1986) calls the prevailing practices for justification of investment in modern manufacturing technology " justification by faith."

The need for appropriate approaches to measure the benefits of modern technologies has become critical. For example, based on an annual survey of large manufacturers in Northern America, Europe and Japan, Tombak and Meyer (1988) and Meyer et al. (1989) conclude that American firms are lagging behind in their efforts to develop efficient methods for evaluating tradeoffs between manufacturing flexibility and cost efficiency. Meredith and Suresh (1986) observe that the absence of adequate methods for justification of modern technology choices leads to rejection of many worthwhile projects. These observations are consistent with those of Jaikumar (1986), who found that, in comparison with the Japanese, U.S. manufacturers installed fewer flexible systems and then failed to use them correctly. This is partly due to high costs of acquisition for flexible systems, and partly due to a lack of appropriate evaluation methods.

SECTION 2.2.2 MODELING APPROACHES WITH A SINGLE PRODUCT

The issue of technology management has become particularly relevant to operations planners in recent years as a result of the introduction of new computer-aided process technologies. In order to select from a set of available technologies, management must develop systematic procedures for analyzing the alternatives and determining relevant tradeoffs. In the remainder of this section I describe a number of models and paradigms that have been developed in the fields of operations management, management science, and economics to address issues related to these topics.

The best known single-product model has been provided by Manne (1961, 1967), who examined the planning problem with linearly increasing demand and stationary costs (except for discounting) over an infinite horizon. The basic tradeoff in this model is between economies of scale in investment costs (represented by concave cost functions) and the benefits due to delay in capacity additions. Manne's main result is that an optimal policy requires additions to capacity at regular intervals. This implies that capacity is added by building plants of fixed size, and that the planning problem reduces to a determination of the optimal plant size (or alternately, the frequency of capacity additions). Figure 2.2.2 shows the process of demand growth and capacity expansion over time. It is interesting to note the similarity between the amount of excess capacity and inventory in an EOQ (economic order quantity) model. Using Manne's characterization, the total discounted cost over the infinite horizon can be expressed as a function of the frequency of capacity addition in the following manner:

$$C(x) = \frac{f(xD)}{1-e^{-rx}} \tag{1}$$

where D = annual increase in demand (units/year)/year
  x = time interval between successive plants (years)
  r = annual discount rate, compounded continuously, (1/year)
  f(·) = investment cost function

The optimal plant size (xD) and the corresponding frequency of capacity additions (x) is determined by minimizing (1). For the special case in which investment cost function is the power function (described in Section 2.1), optimal x = x* is obtained as a solution to the following transcendental equation:

$$\alpha\,(e^{rx^*} - 1) = rx* \tag{2}$$

It is interesting to note that the frequency of capacity additions depends only on the discount rate (r) and the economy of scale parameter (α) and is independent of the magnitude of demand growth (D). The solution for (2) can be simplified by tabulating the values of x* as a function of r and α.

Srinivasan (1967) extended Manne's results to the case in which demand growth is geometric rather than linear. Using an approach similar to that of Manne, Srinivasan showed that it is still optimal to construct plants at constant intervals of time. However, because of the geometric growth in demand, the plant sizes will not remain constant but will grow exponentially.

The continuous time models described so far suffer from two major drawbacks that make them appropriate only for a rough-cut analysis: First, as noted in our discussion of Figure 2.1b, demand growth may not always follow a regular (e.g., a linear or geometric) pattern. Second, standardization of plants and equipment may restrict choices to a few discrete alternatives. To address these and other related issues, a number of finite-horizon, discrete-period models have been developed in the literature. In fact, the choice of discrete time periods poses no problem since the interval lengths can be as small as needed. In fact, discrete time models with interval lengths of a quarter or of a year are consistent with the budget practices of most firms.

One of the earliest finite horizon models is that of Manne and Veinott (1967), who consider the capacity planning problem with general demand growth. However, they assume that the size of capacity additions is unrestricted. This model is identical to that developed by Wagner and Whitin (1958) in the context of lot sizing in production planning. Work related to capacity planning with discrete alternatives has been reported by Erlenkotter (1973a, 1973b) and Neebe and Rao (1983), among others. In what follows, I discuss in detail Neebe and Rao's model (1983). My objective is to describe the scope of such models and to provide the reader with a flavor of the research in this area.

Notation:

T: planning horizon

I: a finite set of n expansion projects, $I = \{1,..., n\}$

z_i: capacity of project i. $z_i > 0$ and may be brought on stream at the start of any period t ($t = 1, 2,..., T$)

c_{it}: investment cost for project i in period t

d_t: demand in period t, $t = 1, 2,..., T$

R_t: $\max\limits_{\tau=1,t} d_\tau$

r_t: the incremental demand in period t,

$$r_t = \max\{0, d_t - R_{t-1}\}$$

$$x_{it} = \begin{cases} 1 & \text{if project i is set at the start of period t} \\ 0 & \text{otherwise} \end{cases}$$

y_t: idle capacity in period t

[NR]

$$\text{min: } \sum_{i=1}^{n} \sum_{t=1}^{T} c_{it}x_{it}$$

subject to:

$$\sum_{t=1}^{T} x_{it} \leq 1 \qquad i \in I \qquad\qquad (3)$$

$$\sum_{i=1}^{n} z_i x_{it} + y_t - y_{t+1} = r_t \qquad t = 1, 2,..., T \qquad (4)$$

$$\sum_{i=1}^{n} x_{it} \leq 1 \qquad t = 1, 2,..., T \qquad (5)$$

$$x_{it} = 0 \text{ or } 1 \qquad i \in I, t = 1, 2,..., T \qquad (6)$$

$$y_t \geq 0 \qquad t = 1, 2,..., T \qquad (7)$$

In the formulation above, (3) ensures that each project can be selected at most once over the planning horizon and (4) guarantees that demand is satisfied in each period. Constraint (5) restricts the number of projects chosen in each period. Note that this model is useful not only in project selection but also in choosing technologies. In the latter case, a project can model technology choice with a specified capacity. For technologies with alternative capacity choices, as many projects as necessary may be defined.

Neebe and Rao considered a special case of [NR] with integral demands and capacities. While the resulting integer program is not particularly amenable for obtaining optimal solution, it allows the authors to develop a Lagrangian relaxation procedure that it is effective for moderate-sized problems that are representative of real-life applications. It is also interesting to note that the NR model is sparse in data requirements. Furthermore, it is consistent with accounting methods and costs c_{it} can be modified to incorporate the cash flows associated with each project. Finally, the model can also be easily modified to capture capacity additions in a phased manner.

2.2.2.1 MULTI-REGION MODEL

When demand is distributed over a geographical area and transportation costs are substantial, it might be economical to build a large number of small plants--each located close to a different market area. The smaller plants would be unable to take advantage of economies-of-scale in manufacturing, but would be able to serve their local markets at low transportation costs.

The single-region models described in the previous section provide a natural starting point and motivate extensions to research on multiple regions. For example, Erlenkotter (1967, 1975) examined the two-region, infinite horizon problem with linear demand growth and characterized the structure of the optimal expansion plans. Based on these properties, he developed an efficient dynamic programming formulation and algorithms for deriving optimal investment plans. Extensions to the multiple region problem are described in Erlenkotter (1975). Fong and Rao (1975) considered the two-region problem with general demand patterns and used a discrete-time, finite-horizon model to address the tradeoffs between scale economies and transportation costs. Using a network representation of the problem, they provided efficient algorithms to obtain optimal solutions.

However, the above procedures do not extend to multiple-region problems, and the focus of subsequent research has shifted to the development of heuristics because of the complex computations involved in seeking exact optimal solutions. In the following sections, I describe, in detail, the model and the results in Fong and Srinivasan (1981a, 1981b, 1986) to illustrate these developments.

Notation:

L: the set of time periods

I : the set of producing regions

I': the same set as I except that it has one more dummy supply region

K: the sets of markets

K': the same set as K except that it has one more dummy supply region

x^t_{ik}: amount shipped from region i to market k during period t

c^t_{ik}: the unit cost of production in region i, a given constant for shipment shipment to market k in period t

z^t_i: amount of capacity expansion in region i in period t

$f^t_i(z^t_i)$: investment cost for establishing a capacity of size z^t_i at region i in period t

q^0_i: initial capacity at region i

d^t_k: demand in region k in period t, a known constant

Model:

[FS]   Min: $\sum\limits_{t\in L}\sum\limits_{i\in I'}\sum\limits_{k\in K'} c^t_{ik}x^t_{ik} + \sum\limits_{i\in L}\sum\limits_{i\in I'} f^t_i(z^t_i)$

subject to:

$$\sum_{k\in K'} x^t_{ik} = q^0_i + \sum_{\tau=1}^{t} z^\tau_i \quad \text{for } i \in I', t \in L \quad (8)$$

$$\sum_{i\in I'} x^t_{ik} = d^t_k \quad\quad\quad \text{for } k \in K', t \in L \quad (9)$$

$$x^t_{ik}, z^t_i \geq 0 \quad \text{for } i \in I', k \in K', t \in L \quad (10)$$

In the above model, the constraints (8) state that the total shipment (including the shipment to the dummy market) from region i at period t must be equal to the initial capacity plus the cumulative expanded capacity up to period t. (9) ensures that the supply from all regions (including the dummy supply) satisfies the demand in market k at period t.

The model FS is a multi-period version of the capacitated warehouse location problem and thus belongs to the class of NP-hard problems. Since the prospect of developing efficient algorithms to obtain optimal solutions for such problems is not very encouraging, Fong and Srinivasan focus on heuristics to derive "good" expansion schedules. In the first stage an initial solution is obtained by solving a sequence of transportation problems that represent one-period versions of FS. In the second stage, improvements are obtained by considering movements of capacity expansions among regions and/or time periods. Essentially, the improvements are myopic in nature and it may be noted that these heuristics evolved from the earlier work of Hung and Rikkers (1974) and Rao and Rutenberg (1977).

It is interesting to note that the multi-region model (FS) can be modified to capture some of the issues related to technology selection in a multi-product environment. This may be done by defining regions to represent products and investments in a region in order to denote use of dedicated technology for that product. Transportation costs may be used to capture product mix flexibility characteristics and to define conversion costs. While this scheme is attractive in principle, I note

that its application is rather limited. This is primarily due to the fact
that the heuristics of Fong and Srinivasan do not extend to more general
cases and thus additional research is required to deal with these features.
For a further elaboration of these aspects, I refer the reader to Chapter 3
in this study, or to Li and Tirupati (1990a).

2.2.2.2 MODELS WITH TECHNOLOGY IMPROVEMENT

Continuing and, in some cases, dramatic improvements in
technology are key characteristics in electronics, semiconductor,
computer and other high technology industries. Investments in new
technologies in these industries have been motivated primarily by
technical breakthroughs in process technologies and by the presence of
competition rather than rational economic analyses. This is partly due
to the lack of suitable models with which to address issues related to
technology improvement. The literature on this topic has been limited.
In this section, I provide a brief overview of the modeling literature on
the subject.

Hinomoto (1965) presented one of the earliest models that
explicitly incorporate technology improvements. Hinomoto considers
two forms of improvement: (a) reduction in investment costs and (b)
reduction in input requirements, which in turn lead to reductions in
operating costs. These features are modeled in the following manner:

(a)   Investment Cost:
Let $K(z)$ denote the cost of adding z units of capacity at time 0. The
corresponding cost for addition at time t is then given by $K(z)e^{-kt}$. The
factor e^{-kt} captures the effect of technology improvement, and $k > 0$ is
the improvement constant.

(b)   Operating Cost:
The operating cost consists of two components--number of units of
input required and the price of the input. The product of the two terms
results in operating costs. Hinomoto assumes that unit price of the
input is exogenously specified by a dynamic function, $q(t)$. The input
requirements depend on the production level (y) and capacity (z), and are
specified by a production function $X[y, z]$. The production function is
defined with the technology at time 0 as the reference. Reductions in
requirements due to technological improvements are modeled in a
manner similar to investment costs with an improvement rate h. Thus

operating cost at time t due to production level $y(t)$ with a capacity z installed at time t_1 is given by $q(t)X[y(t), z]e^{-ht_1}$.

In Hinomoto's model, there are no explicit restrictions on demand and it is assumed that all production is sold. However, the unit price of the product is a function of the total production and the demand process is thus modeled indirectly. It is interesting to note that the model permits a dynamic price function. In the simplest case--termed as one-step model--Hinomoto examines the problem with exactly one opportunity to invest in new capacity. The initial conditions are specified by the age and amount of capacity available at time 0. The objective is to determine (a) the amount and the time of new investment, (b) the optimal length of the production interval (planning horizon), and (c) the production plan during this horizon. It is interesting to note that with this specification, the planning horizon can be partitioned into two periods (of possibly unequal lengths)--before and after the investment in new technology. The two periods are referred to as Period 0 and Period 1, and within each period capacity remains constant. I now describe the model in detail.

Let
n: number of alternative technologies
t_0: purchase time of the existing facility ($t_0 < 0$)
t_1: time the new facility is purchased
z_0: the size of the existing facility
z_1: the size of new facility
$y_0(t)$: the total amount of production at time t in period 0
$y_1(t)$: the total amount of production at time t in period 1
$y_{1,1}(t)$: the amount produced by the new facility at time t
T: planning horizon
r: discount factor

Hinomoto developed the profit function for the one step model as follows:

$$G = \int_0^{t_1} e^{-rt} \{P[y_0(t), t]y_0(t) - q(t)X[y_0(t), z_0] e^{-ht_0}\} dt$$

$$+ \int_{t_1}^{T} e^{-rt}[P[y_1(t), t]y_1(t)] - q(t)\{X[y_1(t) - y_{1,1}(t), z_0] e^{-ht_0}$$

$$+ X[y_{1,1}(t), z_1] e^{-ht_1}\}]dt - K(z_1)e^{-(r+k)t_1} \qquad (11)$$

In (11), the first term represents the net profit from period 0 to t_1, the second term represents the revenue from t_1 to T less operating costs of existing capacity and new facility, and the third term is the investment cost at time t_1. Thus G denotes the present value of the discounted profit. For cases in which G can be treated as a continuous function of the decision variables (T, t_1, z_1, $y_0(t)$, $y_1(t)$, $y_{1,1}(t)$), Hinomoto derives first-order conditions that are necessary for optimality. He also provides an economic interpretation for these conditions and develops some interesting characterizations of the relationship between these variables. While it is not easy to obtain closed-form expressions for optimal values of the decision variables, it is rather straightforward to solve the necessary conditions and obtain numerical values in specific instances. (Several standard computer programs may be used in these computations.) I note that the necessary conditions are sufficient for optimality for cases in which the profit function G is strictly concave.

In recent years, work related to technology choice in the presence of improvement has been reported in the context of both monopolistic and competitive situations. For example, Klincewicz and Luss (1985) examined timing decisions for introduction of new technology facilities. They first examined linearly growing demand and then extended the analysis to nonlinear demand. Boyd et al. (1982) developed a model of the share of an energy product market served by each technology of a set of competing technologies. The objective is to minimize product cost. Gaimon (1986) developed an optimal control model in which the strategic decision concerning the optimal acquisition of flexible technology is examined. Specifically, the model focuses on a profit-maximizing firm and optimally derives its prices, level of output, and its level and composition of productive capacity over time. Gaimon (1989) considered competition between two firms and examined the resulting impact on new technology adoption and capacity addition.

2.2.2.3   MODELS WITH STOCHASTIC DEMAND

The literature on technology evaluation models with stochastic demand is quite sparse and fairly recent. Some of the early work in this area is that of Freidenfelds (1980), and of Whitt and Luss (1981). Freidenfelds showed that when the demand process is a time-homogeneous Markov process and capacity expansion cost is time-invariant, the stochastic model can be reformulated as an equivalent deterministic model. Whitt and Luss computed capacity utilization when demand growth follows geometric Brownian motion. The demand process in these models is quite specialized and has limited potential for application. More recently, Cohen and Halperin (1986) examined a more general model (CH) that considers technology alternatives as well. In this section, I describe this model in some detail.

In the CH model, the authors use a discrete-period, finite-horizon model to examine the tradeoffs between alternative technologies. Each technology is characterized by a dynamic purchase cost and an age-dependent salvage value. The operating costs are comprised of a fixed component and a variable cost that is linear in production volume. In addition, the capacity of each alternative is specified so that capacity decisions are not included in this model.

An interesting feature of the CH model is a provision for dynamic demands. The demand process is described by the specification of a probability density function and a cumulative distribution function for each period. The unit price is assumed to be deterministic, but need not be constant over the planning horizon. Cohen and Halperin (1986) do not permit carry-over of inventories and/or shortages between periods. Instead, shortages due to inadequate production lead to loss of revenue and potential profit. Likewise, excess production gives rise to inventories that cannot be used and incur unnecessary operating costs.

A key feature of the CH model is the assumption that only one type of technology may be used in each period. Furthermore, as described earlier, technology choice defines the available capacity. Thus changes in technology and/or capacity require retirement of existing capacity and investment in a new facility. These rather restrictive assumptions make the model unrealistic and limit its application.

Formally, the objective in the CH model is to maximize the expected profit over the planning horizon. The following notation is useful in describing the details of the model:

Notation:
n: number of alternative technologies
z_i: annual production volume in year i
D_i: annual demand in year i (a random variable)
$F_i(\cdot)$: cumulative distribution of demand in year i
$f_i(\cdot)$: probability density function of demand in year i
r_i: revenue per unit in year i
A_i: the set of technology alternatives available in year i
K_α: annual fixed cost associated with technology α
V_α: unit variable cost for technology α
$S_\alpha(t)$: salvage value at age t for technology α

$C_\alpha{}^i$: purchase cost of technology α in year i

$\gamma = 1/(1+\rho)$: the annual discount factor with discount rate ρ

The evolution of the CH model with uncapacitated technology alternatives may be described in three steps. First, note that a single-period version of the model reduces to n newsboy problems. Thus for a given production technology (say, α) in period i, the optimal production volume is given as

$$z_i{}^*(\alpha) = F_i{}^{-1}[\frac{(r_i - V_\alpha)}{r_i}] \tag{12}$$

The corresponding profit $\Pi_i(\cdot)$ may be computed as follows:

$$\Pi_i(z_i{}^*(\alpha), \alpha) = r_i \{ \int_0^{z_i{}^*(\alpha)} u\, f_i(u)du$$

$$+ z_i{}^*(\alpha)[1- F_i(z_i{}^*(\alpha))]\} - K_\alpha - V_\alpha z_i{}^*(\alpha) \tag{13}$$

It is interesting to note that once the technology is given, the fixed cost K_α does not figure in the production volume. However, it is included in the profit function. For the one-period problem, the technology that maximizes $\Pi_i(z_i{}^*(\alpha), \alpha)$ represents the optimal choice. A negative value for the corresponding $\Pi_i(\cdot)$ implies that the product is not profitable to produce.

Extension of the above model to multiple periods constitutes the second phase in the CH model. Thus given the technology (α) to be used over a finite number of periods (say, from i through j - 1, j > i), the objective is to determine the production levels in each of the periods i, i+1, . . . , j - 1. Again, the goal is to maximize profits over this time interval. Since the capacity of each alternative is well-defined and fixed, the corresponding profit function ($P_{ij}(\alpha)$) is computed rather easily by solving (j - i) one-period problems, and can be expressed as follows:

Let $P_{ij}(\alpha)$ denote maximum expected discount profit associated with using technology $\alpha \in A_i$ from periods i through j - 1 plus the discounted salvage value for α which is received in period j when it is of age j-i. Then

$$P_{ij}(\alpha) = \sum_{t=i}^{j-1} \gamma^t \Pi_t(z_t^*(\alpha), \alpha) + \gamma^i S_\alpha(j - i) \qquad (14)$$

Computation of $P_{ij}(\alpha)$ for all feasible i, j combinations for each technology is done via a dynamic programming formulation of the problem considered by Cohen and Halperin (1986). (The reader may note that this third phase can also be described as a shortest path problem.) The recursive relation for a backward algorithm can be described as follows:

Let $W(i, \alpha)$ denote the profit realized by following an optimal policy from period i through T, given technology α is used in period i

$$W(i, \alpha) = \max_{\substack{j>i \\ \beta \in A_j}} \{P_{ij}(\alpha) - \gamma^j C_\beta^j + W(j, \beta)\} \qquad (15)$$

with $W(T, \cdot) = 0$

In addition to developing a solution procedure, Cohen and Halperin (1986) present an analysis to derive some qualitative insights for the technology choice problem in this restrictive environment. For example, they provide conditions under which it is not economical for a firm to switch to a technology with higher variable costs. Likewise, they also show that a switch-over to a technology with lower variables costs depends on the probability distributions of demand, the relationship of selling price to variable cost, and the relationship of fixed cost to contribution margin. The authors also extended their model to the case of finite capacity and inventory holding and shortage cost.

2.2.3 MODELING APPROACHES WITH TWO PRODUCTS

The presence of multiple products introduces several pertinent issues that further complicate the technology selection problem. These relate to the alternative technologies available, to product mix characteristics, and to demand patterns. To obtain insights into the relevant tradeoffs, researchers focused on the two-product problem and the results parallel the single-product case described in the previous section. The multiple-product problem with more than two products (described in Section 2.2.4) is considerably more complex, and as a result the contributions relate to the development of heuristics and approximation procedures.

As noted earlier, three types of technology describe the alternatives available for the two-product case: (i) dedicated technology capable of producing one product; (ii) flexible technology that can produce both products; and (iii) convertible technology that may be converted from one product to another. It is pertinent to note that the term "flexible technology" may be defined in two ways: (a) as technology, such as flexible manufacturing systems (FMS), that is capable of producing the two products, or (b) as technology specialized for producing one product, but that can be used to meet the demand of another. I now describe some key results that have been obtained in the context of two products.

2.2.3.1 MODELS WITH DETERMINISTIC DEMAND

As in the single-product case, early work examining capacity planning issues with two products focused on the infinite horizon problem with linearly growing demands. For example, Kalotay (1973) considered the problem with dedicated technology designed for one of the products, and with flexible technology designed for both products. Kalotay's analysis does not provide an optimal solution to the problem, but presents lower bounds and characteristics of the optimal plan. Subsequently, Erlenkotter (1974) and Freidenfelds (1981) developed exact (dynamic programming) and heuristic methods respectively to solve the technology selection and capacity planning problem. A variant of this problem with convertible technologies has been examined by Kalotay (1975), Merhaut (1975), and Wilson and Kalotay (1976). In this problem, in addition to investments in new capacities, the key decisions relate to timing and amount of conversion of technology.

In a series of articles, Luss (1979, 1980) examined the two-product finite horizon problem using a discrete period model. The model, which provides for convertible technologies, is formulated in the following manner:

Notation:
i: index for product families, $i = 1, 2$
d_{it}: demand i in period t, a known constant

R_{it}: max $d_{i\tau}$
       $\tau = 1, t$
r_{it}: incremental demand i at period t, $r_{it} = \max\{0, d_{it} - R_{it-1}\}$

x_{it}: amount of capacity addition of type i in period t (available for use in period t)

y_{it}: amount of capacity of type i converted to the other type in period t

I_{it}: amount of idle capacity of type i at the beginning of period t (or, equivalently, the idle capacity at the end of period t - 1, t = 2, 3, . . . , T + 1)

$c_{it}(x_{it})$: investment cost of x_{it} with $c_{it}(x_{it})$ a concave function

$g_{it}(y_{it})$: conversion cost of y_{it}, $g_{it}(y_{it})$ is a concave function

$h_{it}(I_{it+1})$: holding costs of I_{it+1} from t to period t + 1= with $h_{it}(I_{it+1})$ is a concave function

Model:

[LM]   min: $\{ \sum_{t=1}^{T} \sum_{i=1}^{2} [c_{it}(x_{it}) + g_{it}(y_{it}) + h_{it}(I_{it+1})]$

subject to:

$$I_{it+1} = I_{it} + x_{it} + y_{jt} - y_{it} - r_{it}$$

$$i = 1, 2, j = 1, 2 \ (j \neq i); t = 1, 2,..., T \qquad (16)$$

$$x_{it}, y_{it}, I_{it} \geq 0$$

$$i = 1, 2, j = 1, 2 \ (j \neq i); t = 1, 2,..., T \qquad (17)$$

$$I_{i1} = 0, I_{iT+1} = 0$$

$$i = 1, 2, j = 1, 2 \ (j \neq i); t = 1, 2,..., T \qquad (18)$$

The objective in the formulation above is to minimize the total cost incurred, specifically the investment, conversion and holding costs over the planning horizon. Constraints (16) ensure that product demands are satisfied in each period and define the corresponding unutilized capacity. Luss's major contribution is to show that the model LM is equivalent to a network flow problem. Figure 2.2.3.1 describes this network representation of LM. The arcs pointing into each node represent unutilized capacity in the previous period, as well as expansion and conversion from the other capacity in this period, while the arcs out of each node represent demand, unutilized capacity and conversion into the other capacity in the period.

While the network representation provides a useful structure, the solution to LM is difficult to obtain, due to non-linearities in the cost functions. Using extreme point properties, Luss developed a dynamic programming approach that provides optimal solutions for the planning problem with concave cost functions. As discussed earlier, concave functions are typical for most investments, and hence the solution procedures have significant potential for applications. In concluding this section I note that some recent work has focused on the two-product problem similar to LM with dedicated and flexible technology alternatives. I do not describe these results in this chapter, but refer the reader to Chapter 3, or to Li and Tirupati (1990a) and references therein.

2.2.3.2 MODELS WITH STOCHASTIC DEMAND

Uncertainty in demand introduces one more dimension of complexity to the technology selection problem. The literature on the subject is rather sparse and fairly recent. Analytical approaches that provide for stochastic demand usually employ two simplifying assumptions: (i) linear costs and (ii) static distributions of demand. Thus, in these models scale economies and demand dynamics are ignored. The key decisions in this environment may be described as a two-stage hierarchical process. In the first stage, technology choice and investment decisions are made, while capacity allocation and production decisions constitute the second phase. In a multi-period model with static demands, technology choice is a one-time decision made at the beginning of the planning horizon, while the allocation decisions are made in every period and depend on the realizations of product demands. In this section I describe the model examined by Gupta et al. (1988) to illustrate the approach. Related work can be found in Hutchinson and Holland (1982), Fine and Freund (1990), Fine (1990) and references therein. I also note that similar work has been reported by Dempster et al. (1981) and Lenstra et al. (1984) in an entirely different context of machine selection in a stochastic scheduling environment.

Notation:
α: flexibility parameter, $0 \leq \alpha \leq 1$
A, B, AB(α): index for the two dedicated and the flexible capacities respectively
D_i: demand for product i (i = 1, 2) (random variable)

Q_i: production of type i with flexible capacity (i = 1, 2);

Q: a vector with components of (Q_1, Q_2);

R_i: net profit per unit of product i ($R_i > 0$, $R_1 \geq R_2$);

K_A, K_B: number of units of dedicated capacities purchased

$K_{AB}(\alpha)$: number of units of flexible capacity purchased

C_A, C_B: unit purchase prices of dedicated capacities A, B

$C_{AB}(\alpha)$: unit purchase price of flexible capacity

P_i: production of product i with dedicated capacity (i = 1, 2)

$f_{12}(\cdot)$, $F_{12}(\cdot)$: joint probability density and distribution functions of the demands for products 1 and 2

$f_i(\cdot)$, $F_i(\cdot)$: marginal probability density and distribution functions of the demand for product i, i = 1, 2.

Modeling flexibility characteristics is one of the interesting features of the model examined by Gupta et al. They define a flexibility factor $(T(Q; \alpha))$ to capture loss of capacity in flexible technology due to product switchovers. This factor, which is a function of production levels (Q_1, Q_2) and the flexibility parameter α is defined as follows:

$$T(Q; \alpha) = [(\frac{Q_1}{Q_1+Q_2})^\alpha + (\frac{Q_2}{Q_1+Q_2})^\alpha] \qquad (19)$$

Observe that $T(\cdot)$ can take values between 1 and 2. A value of one for the factor implies complete flexibility and no loss of capacity due to product switchover. A factor of 2 would provide for a 50% loss in capacity. It is interesting to note that if flexible technology is used to produce only one product (either 1 or 2) there is no loss of capacity. The capacity constraint for flexible technology can be described as follows:

$$(Q_1 + Q_2) T(Q; \alpha) \leq K_{AB}(\alpha) \qquad (20)$$

I now describe the complete model below:

Model [GM]:

First Stage Investment Model:

Max: $\psi(\alpha, K_A, K_B, K_{AB}(\alpha)) = - C_A K_A - C_B K_B$

$- C_{AB}(\alpha) K_{AB}(\alpha) + E\{\phi(\alpha, K_A, K_B, K_{AB}(\alpha), D_1, D_2)\}$ (21)

$\phi(\alpha, K_A, K_B, K_{AB}(\alpha), D_1, D_2)$ is defined as the solution to the second stage problem described below. It should be noted that the objective function $\psi(\cdot)$ is an unconstrained nonlinear function except for non-negativity requirements on the value of $\alpha, K_A, K_B, K_{AB}(\alpha)$.

Second Stage Capacity Allocation Model:

$\phi(\alpha, K_A, K_B, K_{AB}(\alpha), D_1, D_2)$

$$= \text{Max:} \sum_{i=1}^{2} R_i(P_i + Q_i)$$

subject to:

$$(P_i + Q_i) \leq d_i \qquad i = 1, 2 \tag{22}$$

$$P_1 \leq K_A \tag{23}$$

$$P_2 \leq K_B \tag{24}$$

$$(Q_2 + Q_2)T(Q; \alpha) \leq K_{AB}(\alpha) \tag{25}$$

$$Q_i, P_i \geq 0 \qquad i = 1, 2 \tag{26}$$

where d_i denote realization of product demands.

Observe that capacity allocation decisions are made after product demands have been observed. Also, in this model these demands need not be completely satisfied and hence represent upper bounds on the amounts that may be sold. Constraints (22) capture this feature of the model. Constraints (23), (24) and (25) guarantee that production amounts in dedicated and flexible technologies cannot exceed their available capacities.

Even with restrictive assumptions, the model GM is not easy to solve optimally. Based on first-order optimality conditions, Gupta et al. derived several relationships between the decision variables. These represent necessary conditions for optimality of the first-stage decisions. They are necessary and sufficient for production and allocation decisions at the second stage. The authors examine in detail the special case with completely flexible technology ($\alpha = 1$ and is no longer a decision variable). For this special case, they provide some useful characterizations of the optimal policy. Flexible and inflexible capacities represent the two extreme policies in this environment. The former policy is optimal if $C_{AB} \leq C_A$, $C_{AB} \leq C_B$ and in that case the two products may be aggregated and treated as one. The latter policy is optimal if $C_{AB} > C_A + C_B$ and in that case the problem decomposes into two newsboy problems. Gupta et al. present several numerical results describing the optimal mix of technology choices for cost parameters within these extremes.

2.2.4 MODELING APPROACHES WITH MULTI-PRODUCTS

The literature dealing with technology selection and capacity planning in a multi-product environment parallels the developments in the two-product case. As indicated earlier, the multi-product models are more complex and, with few exceptions, the focus has been on the development of heuristic and approximation procedures. Thus, it is not surprising that theoretical results characterizing the nature of optimal choices have been few and not particularly insightful. (As explained in detail later in this section, Fine and Freund's model (1990) is an exception, but it involves several simplifying assumptions.)

2.2.4.1 MODELS WITH DETERMINISTIC DEMAND

The single- and two-product models described earlier provide a natural starting point for extensions to multiple products. Thus, most of the work reported on this topic is based on finite-horizon, discrete-period models. Typically, these models provide for dynamic, general demand patterns and alternative technology choices. For example, the LM model described in Section 2.2.3.1. extends to multiple products in a straightforward manner. This extension and other variants of the problem with convertible technologies have been explored in Luss (1983, 1986), and in Lee and Luss (1987). These developments are based primarily on the network representation of the problem, and draw upon the extensive literature in the network optimization area. Chapter 4 develops a model examining the tradeoff between dedicated and flexible technologies in this framework. In what follows, I describe briefly the model in Chapter 4 and some key results from that chapter.

Notation:
N: number of product families
T: planning horizon

i: index for product families and technology choices; technology of
     type i refers to dedicated technology capable of producing items in
     product i, i = 0 refers to flexible technology capable of producing all
     products

X_{it}: amount of capacity addition of type i in period t; X_{i0} the initial
     capacity of type i

Y_{it}: amount of flexible capacity allocated to product family i in
     period t

d_{it}: demand for product family i in period t

$f_{it}(\cdot)$: discounted cost function for capacity type i in period t

Model:

$$[LT] \quad Z_{LT} = \text{Min} \sum_{i=0}^{N} \sum_{t=1}^{T} f_{it}(X_{it})$$

subject to:

$$\sum_{\tau=1}^{t} X_{it} + Y_{it} \geq d_{it} \qquad i = 1, 2,..., N; t = 1, 2,..., T \qquad (27)$$

$$\sum_{i=1}^{N} Y_{it} \leq \sum_{t=0}^{t} X_{0\tau} \qquad t = 1, 2,..., T \qquad (28)$$

$$X_{it} \geq 0 \qquad i = 0, 1,..., N; t = 1, 2,..., T \qquad (29)$$

$$Y_{it} \geq 0 \qquad i = 1, 2,... , N; t = 1, 2,..., T \qquad (30)$$

In this model, constraints (27) state that the dedicated capacity of
technology i plus flexible capacity allocated to product family i should
be sufficient to satisfy the demand in period t. Constraints (28) specify
that the total allocation in flexible capacity cannot exceed the
availability. The objective is to minimize the discounted investment
cost and to determine the optimal mix of dedicated and flexible capacity.
Since the optimal solution involves many complex considerations such
as economies of scale, demand patterns, mix flexibility, etc., the
authors developed a two-phase approach and presented heuristics to
obtain approximately optimal expansion schedule. Their computational
experiments provide many interesting results. For example, their results
suggest that substantial investments in flexible technology can be
economically justified even when they are significantly more expensive

than dedicated technologies. Further, these investments occur early in the planning horizon. The heuristics require modest computational effort, and thus the model can be used to support managerial decisions in examining choices in technologies together with sizing and timing of capacity additions.

2.2.4.2 MODELS WITH STOCHASTIC DEMAND

As mentioned earlier, Fine and Freund (1990) analyze a simple model to examine the tradeoffs between dedicated and flexible technologies in a static environment. Their market model is akin to perfect competition and it is assumed that the firm can sell whatever is produced. The demand uncertainties are captured by the specification of the revenue function for each product. In the simplest case, this is equivalent to specifying product prices. Fine and Freund assume that for each product one of a finite set of discrete alternatives will be realized. Thus the market uncertainties are described by a set of scenarios, each of which is characterized by a probability of realization and a corresponding revenue function for each product. The relevant decisions in this environment may be classified into two categories: (a) strategic decisions dealing with the capacity additions for each type of technology, and (b) capacity allocation and production decisions. The latter are made after demand realizations have been observed, and hence it is necessary to specify, for each scenario, both production levels and the amount of allocation of flexible technology to individual products. I now describe the model in detail:

Notation:
n: number of products
j: index for product families and the corresponding dedicated technology
F: index for flexible technology which can produce all products
K_j: amount of dedicated technologies purchased $j = 1,..., n$
K_F: amount of flexible technology purchased
$r_j(K_j)$: acquisition costs for dedicated technologies
$r_F(K_F)$: acquisition costs for flexible technology
k: number of alternative scenarios
i: index for scenarios

P_i: probability of occurrence of scenario i, $\sum_{i=1}^{k} P_i = 1$

Y_{ij}: production of product j with dedicated technologies in scenario i

Z_{ij}: production of product j using flexible technology in scenario i
$R_{ij}(\cdot)$: revenue function for product j in scenario i
$C_j(Y_{ij})$: production cost function with dedicated technologies
$C_F(Z_{ij})$: production cost function with flexible technology

Model:

[FF]   Maximize: $- r_F(K_F) - \sum_j r_j(K_j) + \sum_i P_i \sum_j \{R_{ij}(Y_{ij}$

$$+ Z_{ij}) - C_j(Y_{ij}) - C_F(Z_{ij})\}$$

subject to:

$$Y_{ij} - K_j \leq 0 \qquad i = 1,..., k; \ j = 1,..., n \qquad (31)$$

$$\sum_j Y_{ij} - K_F \leq 0 \qquad i = 1,..., k \qquad (32)$$

$$Y_{ij} \geq 0, \ Z_{ij} \geq 0 \qquad i = 1,..., k; \ j = 1,..., n \qquad (33)$$

$$K_j \geq 0 \qquad\qquad j = 1,..., n \qquad (34)$$

$$K_F \geq 0 \qquad\qquad (35)$$

The objective in the model is to maximize the total revenue less the investment and production costs. (31) and (32) respectively represent capacity constraints for dedicated and flexible technologies. With linear cost and revenue functions, the model FF reduces to a convex program that is amenable for analysis. Using Kuhn-Tucker conditions, the authors derive several interesting properties and derive results that have policy implications for technology selection. For example, their results help explain the economics of investment in flexible capacity, and the sensitivity of profit function and investment levels to changes in acquisition costs. The model also increases understanding of the advantages of investments in flexible technologies.

2.3 APPLICATIONS IN TECHNOLOGY SELECTION AND CAPACITY EXPANSION

It is interesting to note that several of the models described in the previous section were not mere academic exercises, but were motivated by practical considerations. Thus many of the results have been used for generating long-range plans at the corporate level by large firms, and at the industry level by countries with planned (centralized) economies. In this section I briefly describe some of these applications. The section is organized by industry. For each case, I identify its distinctive characteristics and relate them to the appropriate models and/or results.

Process and Chemical Industry

The process and chemical industry motivated some of the early research on capacity planning. This is a fairly mature industrial sector with homogeneous products and well-established process technologies. The stable product mix permits product aggregation, and single-product models are usually adequate for capacity planning decisions. Technology is highly capital intensive, with significant scale economies and discrete, well-defined alternatives. Thus for a rough-cut analysis, the continuous-time models of Manne (1961, 1967), and Srinivasan (1967) are adequate. For detailed planning involving specific projects, the discrete time models of Erlenkotter (1973), and Neebe and Rao (1983) may be used. Applications of these methods in the aluminium, caustic soda, cement, and fertilizer industries in India have been reported by Manne (1967). Vietorisz and Manne (1963) present a similar study for the synthetic fertilizer industry in Latin America. I note that for cases with spatially distributed demands and significant transportation costs (as in the cement and fertilizer industries) the multi-region model is appropriate.

Communications Industry

In the communications industry some of models described in the previous section have been used in capacity planning of cable production. The cable market may be described as being made up of multiple products with limited substitution. Each cable type is characterized by the diameter of the wire pairs in the cable, and cable size is defined by the number of wire pairs. Cables with larger numbers of wire pairs are more expensive (in terms of investment and operational costs), but can be used to satisfy the demand for cables with fewer wire pairs.

As described in Section 2.2.2, three types of models have been used for capacity planning in this environment. In the simplest cases Kalotay (1973) considered two types of cables and the objective was to develop expansion plans for each cable type. The tradeoff is between scale economies in investment, and demand patterns that make substitution with more expensive cables (for part of the time) economically viable. Subsequent models such as Luss (1979, 1980) permit modifications of technology to convert capacity from one type to the other. In this case, in addition to the factors described earlier, I have to consider the tradeoff between one-time conversion costs and the cost of meeting demand with more expensive cable. Extension of these models to multiple-product types and other related work can be found both in Luss (1983, 1986) and Lee and Luss (1987).

It is interesting but not surprising to note that most of the research in this context had its origins at AT &T Bell Laboratories. And, in most cases, the emphasis was on development of implementable algorithms to facilitate ready application.

Automobile, Fabrication and Discrete Part Manufactures

These industries are characterized by increasing variety in product mix and wide uncertainty in product demands. The technology problem is further complicated by recent developments in modern technologies that provide substantial operational flexibility and a host of incidental benefits. As pointed out in Section 2.2.2, models and analytical tools in this area have not kept pace with market and technological developments. Accordingly, there is substantial scope for modeling and development of evaluation methodology. However, in spite of these weakness, the importance of technology selection has led to some model-based analysis. For example, Burstein (1986) developed a two-product model incorporating productions and choices between flexible and dedicated technology. Hutchinson and Holland (1982) developed a simulation model to examine the tradeoff between flexible manufacturing systems (FMSs) and transfer lines (dedicated technology). Bird (1987) examined capacity changes by investing in new technologies under uncertain demands. The tradeoff is between increasing expected revenue from more facilities, and the costs of additional investments.

Water Resources

Water resources are essential for irrigation, flood control, transportation and recreation. Expansion of water resource systems requires substantial investments in various projects such as dams, reservoirs, and canals. Erlenkotter (1973) examined the problem of finding the sequence of a finite set of expansion projects to meet a deterministic demand projection at minimum discounted cost. If each project is considered as one particular type of technology, the water resource problem is equivalent to the problem of selecting technologies to satisfy demand. Other related work can be found in Butcher et al. (1969), Young et al. (1970), Jacoby and Loucks (1972), Morin and Esogbue (1971), and Erlenkotter (1973a, 1973b, 1975, 1976).

2.4 CONCLUSION

In this chapter I have discussed the key factors of the capacity planning and technology selection problem, and have described some basic analytical models that have been developed to support these strategic decisions. The discussion in this chapter should make it clear to the reader that a considerable amount of methodology has been developed in the literature to address a variety of issues associated with technology choice, equipment selection, and capacity planning. It is interesting to note that much of this work was motivated by practical considerations, and that several of the results presented in this chapter have been successfully applied in the making of related strategic choices. While the literature on capacity planning and technology selection is quite extensive, it is also clear that most of the models do not adequately capture the key characteristics associated with technologies such as CIM and FMS in the discrete part manufacturing industry.

III. TECHNOLOGY CHOICE AND CAPACITY EXPANSION WITH TWO-PRODUCT FAMILIES: TRADEOFFS BETWEEN SCALE AND SCOPE

In recent years, flexible technology has emerged as a critical need for operations managers. Undoubtedly, this need stems from an increasingly competitive marketplace that is characterized, among other things, by dynamic and uncertain demands, changing product mixes, and short product life cycles. Perhaps this explains why many firms have invested in various advanced technologies such as Computer Aided Design (CAD), Computer Aided Manufacturing (CAM), Computer Integrated Manufacturing (CIM) and Flexible Manufacturing Systems (FMS) that provide operational flexibility in order to satisfy customer requirements. In general, flexible technology systems can produce different types of products with almost negligible set-up time and cost. In contrast, systems with dedicated technology are specially designed to produce a limited product mix. Flexible technologies are often more costly to acquire and to install than are dedicated technologies. However, these modern technologies provide additional benefits that include economies of scope, and the capability to increase manufacturing flexibility, enhance productivity, improve quality, reduce lead times, and decrease inventory levels. These characteristics are particularly useful in meeting dynamic and uncertain demands in the market.

The experience of an automobile manufacturer described in Gerwin (1989) illustrates the potential impact of flexible technologies. In this case, perhaps motivated by a desire to produce at a low cost, the firm made a decision to invest plants with dedicated technology. Later, the demand for some new models was higher than the forecasts. But the company could not take advantage of this opportunity even though some capacity on other lines was available. Gerwin cites this example to suggest that in such situations flexible technology could provide a hedge against uncertainty with its ability to produce several products.

This product mix flexibility, which is also referred to as economies of scope, could play a similar role even in situations with little or no uncertainty. For example, consider the case of the consumer electronics industry, which has dynamic product mixes due to short product life cycles, as well as the constant introduction of new products and retirement of old items. Clearly, scope economies could be an important advantage in such cases.

While most managers have a good conceptual understanding of the uses and benefits of flexible technology, studies indicate that in comparison to Japanese manufacturers, U.S. companies have installed fewer flexible manufacturing systems (Jaikumar (1986)). This is partly due to the high acquisition costs of flexible technology and partly due to the lack of appropriate evaluation methods for making such choices. Currently, firms in the U.S. make their investments with either inadequate, or no, justification.

Nevertheless, the problem is complex and involves a study of several factors such as economies of scale and scope, dynamic and uncertain demands, and manufacturing flexibility. Popular methods such as NPV (net present value) and IRR (internal rate of return) provide marginal analysis and are not directly suitable for the evaluation of the benefits of manufacturing flexibility. The literature in capacity expansion considers scale economies and dynamic demands, but product mix flexibility provided by systems such as CIM and FMS is not captured in these models. While some recent work on economic evaluation of flexibility examines the tradeoffs between dedicated and flexible technologies under deterministic or uncertain demands, the issues of scale economies and dynamic demands are not considered in any detail. (See Section 3.1 for a detailed review of the literature.)

In this chapter, I examine issues related to investments in flexible technology in the context of a firm manufacturing two families of products. The objective is to develop a capacity expansion plan to satisfy the forecast demand over a finite planning horizon. In developing such a plan, the firm has to evaluate alternative technologies and specify the amount of capacity additions of each type in each period. Thus, it is necessary to determine the optimal mix of technologies and expansion schedules so as to minimize the total investment cost over the planning horizon. Since the resulting optimization model is difficult to solve, my focus is on the development of heuristics to provide good solutions with reasonable effort. My computational results show that these solution procedures perform very well. The heuristic solutions are very close to the respective optimal solutions, with average errors typically less than 1.0 %.

The chapter is organized as follows: Section 3.1 provides a brief review of related research. In Section 3.2 I describe the capacity planning problem in detail and discuss two alternative formulations. Sections 3.3 and 3.4 focus on solution procedures and on the derivation of bounds on the performance of the heuristics. The results of computational experiments to illustrate the application of the heuristics are described in Section 3.5. I conclude in Section 3.6 with a brief discussion of the scope of the model and its extensions to address related issues.

3.1   LITERATURE REVIEW

Early work in capacity expansion focused on the single-product case with variations in demand patterns, planning horizons, and cost functions. For example, Manne (1961, 1967) examined the problem with linearly increasing demand and stationary costs (except for discounting) over an infinite horizon. Srinivasan (1967) extended Manne's model to cases with geometric growth in demand. Manne and Veinott (1967) used a discrete time period model to examine the expansion problem with arbitrary growth in demand over a finite horizon.

Following the initial work described above, a considerable amount of literature has been reported on the two product cases. Kalotay (1973) presented a mathematical analysis for a capacity expansion problem involving two classes of linearly growing demands and two types of capacity. The less expensive dedicated capacity could serve only one class of demand, but the more expensive "flexible" capacity could serve both classes of demands. The objective was to find an expansion policy that would minimize total discounted investment costs over an infinite horizon. Erlenkotter (1974) developed a dynamic programming approach to solve the problem. To reduce the computational burden, Freidenfelds (1981) presented several heuristics to obtain approximate solutions.

A variant of the two-product problem has been considered by Merhaut (1975). In this model, there exist two types of capacity, standard and deluxe. Each type of capacity can produce one class of demand. The deluxe capacity can be converted (with some conversion cost) to the standard capacity to produce that demand. Once the deluxe capacity is converted, it becomes an integral part of the standard capacity and cannot be reconverted to the deluxe capacity. Kalotay (1975) and Wilson and Kalotay (1976) extended Kalotay's mathematical analysis to Merhaut case. Luss (1979, 1980) considered another variant of the problem in which the capacity of each type can be converted into the other type at some conversion cost. In addition, this model differs from the others in several respects. These include (i) provision for arbitrary but growing demand patterns, (ii) finite horizons, and (iii) discrete time periods. The problem is formulated as a network model. Extensions to more than two products have been explored by Luss (1983, 1986), and Lee and Luss (1987). For a comprehensive review of the literature prior to 1982, the reader is referred to Luss (1982).

In recent years, there has been a growing body of literature focusing on the choice of flexible technology as a competitive weapon. For instance, Hutchinson and Holland (1982) and Burstein (1986) have studied tradeoffs between modularity and convertibility of flexible technology and the indivisibility ("lumpiness") of dedicated systems as a basis for selecting an optimal mix of rigid and flexible automation. They assume that the demand for each product family is stationary. Fine and Freund (1990) and Gupta et al. (1988, 1990) have recently examined investments and tradeoffs between flexible and dedicated technologies in situations with static, but uncertain, demands. They formulate the problem as a two-stage stochastic program in which the investment decisions are made in the first stage, and the production allocation decisions are made in the second stage. Fine and Freund (1990) consider the two-product case and develop results to characterize the nature of optimal policies. Gupta et. al. (1988, 1990) define an index to describe the degree of flexibility, and use it to examine the benefit of flexibility in the multiple-product case. For further details of related work, we refer the reader to an excellent review by Fine (1989) and references therein.

In contrast to the earlier work in capacity planning (see Luss (1979, 1980), I consider flexible capacity as an alternative to dedicated capacities for producing two- product families. While most models use linear and static investment cost functions, our model permits economies-of-scale in capacity additions and dynamic cost functions. This feature is particularly useful since new and advanced technologies usually tend to exhibit substantial economies-of-scale (see Tang (1989)) and are likely to result in cost reduction. In addition, I permit dynamic and general demand patterns. Incorporation of all these features result in optimization problems (concave minimization) that are difficult to solve. Hence, my focus on the development of heuristics to derive near-optimal solutions with reasonable computational effort.

3.2   THE CAPACITY PLANNING PROBLEM

I consider a capacity planning problem faced by a firm manufacturing a number of products grouped into two-product families. I assume that the demand for each family is known and specified over the planning horizon. This model is quite general and permits a wide variety of demand patterns. This feature is particularly useful in capturing, within each family, the dynamics associated with product life cycles, introduction of new items, and phasing out of obsolete products. The investment planning problem examined in this chapter deals with the choice of technology and additions of capacity to meet the demand for each family. I assume that the demand for each family may be satisfied by (i) dedicated plants designed to produce one-product family or (ii) plant with flexible technology or (iii) a combination of (i) and (ii). The objective is to minimize the total discounted investment cost in both flexible and dedicated plants over a planning horizon.

For the sake of simplicity in the presentation, I assume that the variable production costs for each family do not depend on the type of technology used, and thus omit these costs from the model. However, this is not a serious limitation and the model can be modified to incorporate these aspects. If these costs are linear, the solution procedures presented in this paper will extend in a straightforward manner. Linear production costs are typical of several industries (see Manne (1967), and Fong and Rao (1975)).

We formulate the strategic investment planning model as follows:

Notation:

i: index for technologies and product families. $i = 1$ and 2 refer to the two product families and dedicated technologies. $i = 0$ refers to the flexible technology.

d_{it}: the forecast demand for product family i in period t, $i = 1$ and 2; $t = 1, 2,..., T$.

X_{it}: the amount of technology i acquired at the beginning of the period t, $i = 0, 1, 2$; $t = 1, 2,..., T$.

X_{i0}: initial capacity of technology i.

Y_{it}: the amount of flexible capacity allocated to product family i in period t, $i = 1, 2$; $t = 1, 2,..., T$.

$f_{it}(\cdot)$: the investment cost function for addition of capacity type i in period t, $i = 0, 1, 2$; $t = 1, 2,..., T$.

$$[CP] \quad Z_{CP} = \text{Min} \sum_{i=1}^{2} \sum_{t=1}^{T} f_{it}(X_{it}) + \sum_{t=1}^{T} f_{0t}(X_{0t})$$

subject to:

$$\sum_{\tau=1}^{t} X_{i\tau} + Y_{it} \geq d_{it} \quad i = 1, 2; t = 1, 2,..., T \quad (1)$$

$$\sum_{i=1}^{2} Y_{it} \leq \sum_{\tau=0}^{t} X_{0\tau} \qquad t = 1, 2,..., T \qquad (2)$$

$$X_{it} \geq 0 \qquad i = 0, 1, 2; t = 1, 2,... , T \qquad (3)$$

$$Y_{it} \geq 0 \qquad i = 1, 2; t = 1, 2,..., T \qquad (4)$$

The objective function represents the total cost of capacity additions over the planning horizon. To reflect economies of scale, we assume that $f_{it}(\cdot)$ is concave and strictly increasing. We observe that this a characteristic found in many industries (see Luss (1982)). A discount factor is not explicit in the objective function, but it can be incorporated in the functions $f_{it}(\cdot)$. In our model, stationarity in costs is not necessary, and the functions $f_{it}(\cdot)$ can be defined independently for each i and t. This is a particularly useful feature in modeling new technologies, since advances in technology could lead to cost reductions in the future. Formally, the objective is to minimize the total discounted cost over the planning horizon.

Constraints in (1) specify that capacity (dedicated and flexible) allocated for each product should be sufficient to meet its demand. Constraints in (2) guarantee that allocations of flexible capacity will not exceed availability. Without loss of generality, we assume that initial capacity of dedicated technology is zero, i.e. $X_{i0} = 0$ for i = 1, 2. If the initial capacities are non-zero, the demands d_{it} may be adjusted to be net of the initial capacity. This notion is similar to that of the concept of effective demands used in the context of hierarchical production planning (for example, see Hax and Candea (1984), p.408.). However, this simplification will not apply to flexible technology and we permit initial capacity X_{00} to take positive value.

Note that there is no provision for inventory in this model. This is not a limitation of the models which can be extended to include these decisions. Also, the solution procedures developed in this paper can be modified easily to take into account linear inventory costs. However, I recognize that while building up inventory to meet seasonal demands is a common strategy in short- and medium-term production planning, it does not and should not play a significant role in long-term capacity planning associated with choice of technologies. In models in which inventory is included, the time period is usually long enough (typically a year) to absorb seasonalities in demands. The reader will note that my model is consistent with the decision hierarchy in most firms, where technology choices, capacity expansion, and production planning decisions are made at different levels. As noted in Hax and Meal (1975), this is an important feature that enhances implementation potential of such models.

I note that **CP** includes capacity expansion variables X_{it} and allocation variables Y_{it}. While this represents a "natural" formulation of the planning problem, the model is not consistent with the practices in most firms where the expansion and allocation decisions are made at different stages. Typically, technology choices and expansion alternatives are considered when investment plans are made, and allocation decisions follow in the second stage. Hence, I propose an alternative model **MCP** that does not include the allocation variables, Y_{it}. However, as Proposition 1, below, makes it clear, the two problems are equivalent, and given a feasible solution to **MCP**, it is always possible to find allocations of flexible capacity to satisfy the demand for each product family.

[MCP]

$$Z_{MCP} = \text{Min:} \sum_{i=1}^{2} \sum_{t=1}^{T} f_{it}(X_{it}) + \sum_{t=1}^{T} f_{0t}(X_{0t})$$

subject to:

$$\sum_{\tau=1}^{t} X_{i\tau} + \sum_{\tau=0}^{t} X_{0\tau} \geq d_{it} \qquad i = 1, 2; \ t = 1, 2,..., T \quad (5)$$

$$\sum_{i=1}^{2} \sum_{\tau=1}^{t} X_{i\tau} + \sum_{\tau=0}^{t} X_{0\tau} \geq \sum_{i=1}^{2} d_{it} \qquad t = 1, 2,..., T \quad (6)$$

$$X_{it} \geq 0 \qquad i = 0, 1, 2; \ t = 1, 2,..., T \quad (7)$$

Proposition 1: Problems **CP** and **MCP** are equivalent. (See Appendix A for proof.)

Both **CP** and **MCP** are concave minimization problems with the well-known property that an optimal solution occurs at one of the extreme points of the convex set formed by the constraints. Thus one can restrict one's attention to extreme point solutions. Earlier work (see Fong and Rao (1975), and Luss (1979, 1980, 1986)) made use of this property and the embedded network structures of the problem in developing exact and heuristic algorithms. The inclusion of flexible capacity in my model makes the identification of embedded network structure even harder. Hence, my focus is on the development of heuristics to derive near-optimal expansion schedules. In this chapter, I focus on the **MCP** formulation and examine two related subproblems (referred to as **SP** and **SMCP**) for generating approximate solutions. My approach may be interpreted as a two-stage procedure. In the first stage, an initial feasible solution is obtained by solving a sequence of subproblems. In the second stage, several heuristics are used to improve the initial solution. The details are discussed in the following section.

3.3   INITIAL SOLUTION PROCEDURE

In this section, I describe two approaches for obtaining a feasible solution for MCP. In both methods I use a rolling horizon approach and construct a feasible solution by solving a sequence of subproblems. The subproblems have a shorter planning horizon (say, T_S) and are similar to MCP with some additional restrictions. The objective is to obtain a feasible solution by solving the subproblems optimally with reasonable computational effort.

The rolling horizon procedure requires the solution of $T-T_S+1$ subproblems and works as follows: First, I solve the subproblem defined over the periods one to T_S. However, only the first period investments are included in the initial solution, and represent the initial conditions for the second subproblem that spans periods 2 to T_S+1. The process is repeated until the last problem defined over periods $T-T_S+1$ to T is solved. The initial conditions for this subproblem are defined by the first period investments of the earlier subproblems.

3.3.1   SMCP APPROACH

In this method I propose the use of two-period subproblems to derive a feasible solution. The subproblems are otherwise identical to MCP and are referred to as **SMCP**. The rolling horizon approach requires the solution of (T-1) subproblems to generate a feasible expansion plan. The reader will note that **SMCP** has six variables and six constraints. In my heuristic procedures I rely on the fact that an optimal solution to SMCP may be found at one of the extreme points of the set of feasible solutions. However, even for the two-period SMCP, the maximum number of extreme points is about 900 (This is because we have 6 decision variables, 6 surplus variables, and 6 constraints for a SMCP.) Complete enumeration of these extreme point solutions requires substantial computational effort. Hence, I propose to implicitly examine the extreme points by considering alternative expansion strategies. In Figure 3.3.1 I present a list of such strategies, which together include potential optimal solutions to **SMCP**. (See Figure 3.3.1 for a complete description of the expansion strategies.) Also, each strategy has implications for certain types of investment so that some variables can be set at zero. As a result, the number of extreme points for each strategy is rather small (not greater than ten). Thus I obtain an optimal solution to **SMCP** in the following manner:

(i) For each strategy in Figure 3.3.1, determine the best solution by examining all extreme points.
(ii) The least cost plan among the alternatives generated in step (i) is an optimal solution to **SMCP**.

I developed several alternative expansion strategies to segment the investment possibilities so that examination of extreme points becomes easier. Some extreme cases such as investment in all three technologies in both periods or in the second period are omitted. It is easy to prove that these cases are dominated by alternative strategies. For example, if the two dedicated technologies are to constitute the second period investment, it is not economical to invest in flexible technology since flexible technology is more expensive and investment cost functions for all three technologies are concave.

An example illustrating the application of this procedure is given in Appendix B.

3.3.2 SP APPROACH

In this method the subproblems (referred to as **SP**) have a planning horizon that is larger than that of **SMCP**, but smaller than that of **MCP**. T_S, the planning horizon of **SP**, is a parameter that needs to be specified (this issue is discussed later in this section). **SP** is similar to **MCP** with one additional restriction: at most one investment in each technology is permitted. Clearly, the specification of **SP** is influenced by the need to define tractable computational procedures. The choice of a shorter planning horizon is motivated by the notion that investments in the first period are not unduly affected by the demands in later periods. (The reader will recall that I propose a rolling horizon procedure in which only the first period decisions are implemented). Also, similar results have been obtained in the context of production planning. (For example, see the planning horizon theorem in Lundin and Morton (1975), p.714 and in Hax and Candea (1984), p.76).) The restriction on the number of investments is consistent with this philosophy.

The foregoing discussion suggests that T_S may be a critical parameter for the procedures developed in this section. A low value of T_S may lead to solutions that will result in frequent investments and that will not capture the advantages of economies-of-scale. A large value of T_S may have fewer additions of capacity than necessary. In section 3.5, I empirically examine the impact of T_S on the quality of the solutions. These results suggest that the choice of T_S is not very critical, and that the quality of heuristics are not significantly affected by its value.

I note that even with the additional restrictions, SP is not easy to solve, and I propose an implicit enumeration procedure to determine an optimal solution to SP. Let $SP(t_0, t_1, t_2)$ denote the problem SP, with the specification that investments in technology i may be made only in period t_i, $i = 0, 1, 2$. $t_i = 0$ implies no investment in technology i is permitted.

An algorithm to solve SP:

Initialization: $X_{it} = 0 \; \forall \; i, t$ and the objective value $= \infty$
   For $t_0 = 0, 1,..., T_S$;
      For $t_1 = 0, 1,..., T_S$;
         For $t_2 = 0, 1,..., T_S$;
            Solve the corresponding $SP(t_0, t_1, t_2)$. If $SP(t_0, t_1, t_2)$
            is infeasible, $Z_{SP(t_0, t_1, t_2)} = \infty$. Otherwise, if
            $Z_{SP(t_0, t_1, t_2)} <$ current objective value, then update the
            optimal solution and objective value.
         next t_2.
      next t_1.
   next t_0.

Clearly, solution of $SP(t_0, t_1, t_2)$ is a critical step in the algorithm described above, and in the remainder of this section I discuss the related procedures in detail. Recall that $SP(t_0, t_1, t_2)$ has the same form as MCP except that the planning horizon is T_S instead of T and one additional restriction:

$X_{it} = 0 \qquad t \neq t_i, i = 0, 1, 2; t = 1, 2,..., T_S$ (8)

Elimination of the variables that are assigned zero value (equation 8) results in a specific structure for the constraints of $SP(t_0, t_1, t_2)$ and considerably simplifies the problem. For example, consider the constraints (5) in **MCP** for a specific value of i, say i = 1 for the case $t_0 < t_1$:

$$0 \geq d_{1t} \qquad t = 1, 2,..., t_0\text{-}1 \qquad\qquad (9)$$

$$X_{0t_0} \geq d_{1t} \qquad t = t_0, t_0\text{+}1,..., t_1\text{-}1 \qquad (10)$$

$$X_{0t_0} + X_{1t_1} \geq d_{1t} \quad t = t_1, t_1\text{+}1,..., T_s \qquad (11)$$

Likewise, if $t_0 > t_1$, then constraints may be written as follows:

$$0 \geq d_{1t} \qquad t = 1, 2,..., t_1\text{-}1 \qquad\qquad (12)$$

$$X_{1t_1} \geq d_{1t} \qquad t = t_1, t_1\text{+}1,..., t_0\text{ -}1 \qquad (13)$$

$$X_{0t_0} + X_{1t_1} \geq d_{1t} \quad t = t_0, t_0\text{+}1,..., T_s \qquad (14)$$

For specified values of t_0, t_1 and t_2, constraint (6) and the remaining constraints in (5) (for i = 2) of **MCP** exhibit the same form. Clearly SP(t_0, t_1, t_2) is infeasible if demand for i at the period prior to min$\{t_i$ -1, t_0 -1$\}$ is positive. In such cases, no further analysis is necessary. For problems with feasible solutions, We eliminate redundant constraints in each type (for example, in (10) one constraint will dominate others). As a result, SP(t_0, t_1, t_2) may be formulated as a concave minimization problem with at most seven constraints. This equivalent formulation of SP(t_0, t_1, t_2) may be described as follows:

$$[SP(t_0, t_1, t_2)] \quad Z_{SP}(t_0, t_1, t_2)$$

$$= \text{Min:} \quad \sum_{i=0}^{2} f_{it_i} (X_{it_i})$$

subject to:

$$X_{it_i} \geq d'_i \qquad i = 0, 1, 2$$

$$X_{it_i} + X_{jt_j} \geq d'_{ij} \qquad i = 0; 1, \ j \neq i \text{ and } j \neq 0$$

$$X_{0t_0} + X_{1t_1} + X_{2t_2} \geq d'_{012}$$

$$X_{it_i} \geq 0 \qquad i = 0, 1, 2$$

where d'_i: largest right hand side in constraints of type similar to (10) or (13) for $i = 0, 1, 2$; d'_{ij}: largest right hand side in constraints of type similar to (11) or (14) for $i = 0, 1, j \neq i$ and $j \neq 0$; d'_{012}: largest right hand side in constraints of type of $\sum_{i=0}^{2} X_{it_i} \geq \sum_{i=1}^{2} d_{it}$, $t = t_m, ..., T_s$; t_m: $\max\{t_0, t_1, t_2\}$.

Note that $SP(t_0, t_1, t_2)$ represents the general structure of the problem and that in some instances for specific values of t_0, t_1, t_2, the number of constraints may be smaller than seven. $SP(t_0, t_1, t_2)$ is a tractable concave minimization problem with 3 variables and at most seven constraints and may be solved in several ways. I propose a simple method that is based on the following observations:

(i) In a optimal solution, at least one of the constraints of $SP(t_0, t_1, t_2)$ is binding.
(ii) If the binding constraint is specified, the variables in the problem may be reduced to two and an optimal solution may be obtained by examining all the resulting extreme points.

In my procedure, I set each constraint, one at a time, as an equality and solve the resulting two variable problem. An example to illustrate the procedure is presented in Appendix C.

3.4   IMPROVEMENT HEURISTICS AND LOWER BOUND

3.4.1   IMPROVEMENT HEURISTICS

The improvement methods described in this section constitute the second stage of the heuristics to solve the capacity planning problem. The feasible solution obtained in the first stage becomes the initial candidate solution for the second stage. The basic philosophy at this stage is to generate alternate plans by examining perturbations of the candidate solution. I adopt a greedy approach and choose the alternative leading to largest reduction in the objective function as the next candidate solution. The procedure is repeated until no further improvement is possible. It is easy to terminate this procedure earlier by incorporating upper limits on the number of iterations and/or computational efforts. These improvements heuristics, classified as (i)

Temporal Shift, (ii) Technology Shift, and (iii) Temporal and Technology shift, are described in detail below (see Appendix D for details of the procedures):

(i)   Temporal Shift:

I consider one type of technology at a time, and assume that all investments in other technologies are fixed. Two alternatives to adjust the expansion plans are examined: (a) Global Shift and (b) Forward/Backward Shift.

(a) Global Shift:

The motivation for this heuristic comes from the observation that once expansion plans for all technologies except one (say type i) are specified, an optimal expansion schedule for type i can be derived by solving a related single-product problem. In this problem, I first allocate to product families other than i just enough flexible capacity to meet their respective demands.

The remainder (unused) flexible capacity is used to meet the demands of type i. Any unsatisfied demand for product i after this allocation represents the net demand for technology i. The resulting problem is identical to that examined by Manne & Veinott (1967) and can be solved efficiently.

(b) Forward or Backward Shift:

The heuristic is similar to the one employed by Fong and Srinivasan (1986) in developing algorithms for the single-product multi-region capacity expansion problem. In this method I examine changes in expansion plans within intervals defined by successive capacity additions in the same type of technology. In Forward Shift, I consider intervals in chronological sequence, while in Backward Shift I examine the intervals in reverse order. The objective is to take advantage of scale economies by shifting investments to an earlier or later period without increasing the number of capacity additions.

(ii) Technology Shift:

Here I examine the effect of shifts in capacity between technologies. Technology Shift corresponds to the case in which two or more investments occur in the same period. The heuristic is designed to examine the effect of changes in the mix of capacity additions. In particular I focus on flexible capacity as a substitute for investments in more than one technology.

(iii) Temporal and Technology Shift:

Here I examine an interval defined by successive capacity additions (not necessarily of the same type). I examine changes in technology mix as well as timing of capacity additions. The purpose is to adjust the current expansion schedule to a schedule with a better technology mix and more appropriate investment periods within the interval.

It may be noted that the heuristics described above represent alternative methods to generate incremental changes in the schedule of capacity additions, and may be implemented in several ways. Also, it is not necessary to incorporate all of them in the second phase of the algorithm. Figure 3.4.1 describes my implementation for the numerical examples described in Section 3.5. In this scheme, I alternatively examine temporal and technology shifts until no further improvement is possible.

3.4.2   LOWER BOUND

My aim in this section is to present a simple method to compute a lower bound on Z_{MCP} (the objective function value of MCP) that may be used to establish the quality of the heuristic solutions. The method relies on deriving a cost function for each period that is a lower envelope of the functions $f_{it}(\cdot)$. A lower bound on Z_{MCP} is obtained by solving a one-product problem with this cost function and a demand vector that represents the total demand for all products. The details of the procedure are described below:

Step 1:   For period t (t = 1, 2,..., T), determine aggregate demand, TD_t, as follows: $TD_t = \sum\limits_{i=1}^{N} d_{it}$.

Step 2:   Determine $f_t^*(\cdot)$, the lower bound of the function $f_{it}(\cdot)$, t = 1, 2,..., T, i.e., $f_t^*(\cdot) = \min\limits_{0 \le i \le N} \{ f_{it}(\cdot) \}$.

Step 3.   A lower bound to MCP is obtained by solving the following problem:

$$Z_{WW} = \text{Min} \sum\limits_{t=1}^{T} f_t^*(XA_t)$$

s.t.

$$\sum_{\tau=1}^{t} XA_\tau \geq \sum_{\tau=1}^{t} TD_\tau \qquad t = 1, 2,..., T \qquad (4.1)$$

$$XA_t \geq 0 \qquad\qquad t = 1, 2,..., T \qquad (4.2)$$

where XA_t is aggregate capacity of all technologies at period t. The problem above is equivalent to the one examined in Manne and Veinott (1967) and in Wagner and Whitin (1958), and can be solved by efficient dynamic programming procedures of $O(T^2)$.

While the lower bound procedure described above is easy to compute, the quality of the bound depends on the closeness of the functions f_{it} to the f^*_t. In particular, we expect the lower bound to be poor when: (a) flexible technology is significantly more expensive than dedicated technologies; (b) the demands are so erratic that considerable amounts of flexible technology investment are optimal; and (c) significant scale economies are present.

3.5   COMPUTATIONAL RESULTS

In this section, I report the results of computational experiments to evaluate the quality of the heuristics presented in this paper. In these test problems my objective is to compare the optimal solutions with those obtained by using the **SMCP** and **SP** methods. It is not easy to compute optimal solutions for capacity planning problems with general concave cost functions. Hence, in the test problems I use cost functions of the type referred to as "fixed charge" functions. Thus investment costs are linear in capacity with an additional fixed cost that is independent of amount of capacity addition. The capacity planning problem for this special cost function may be formulated as a mixed zero-one integer programming (see Appendix E for details). I use the **MPSX** mixed-integer programming package to obtain optimal solutions. For each test problem, I also compute the lower bound described in the previous section. Before discussing the computational results, I describe the cost functions and other factors in the design of the test problems.

(i) Investment Cost Functions, $f_{it}(\cdot)$:
In my test problems, the cost functions have the following form:

$$f_{it}(x) = \begin{cases} 0 & \text{if} \quad x = 0 \\ A+Bx & \text{if} \quad x > 0 \end{cases}$$

The use of such functions is quite common, for example, see Luss (1982). In my computational experiments, I used two sets of cost functions as described below:

Set 1: $f_{it}(x) = \begin{cases} r^{t-1}[30+7x] & x>0 \\ 0 & x=0 \end{cases}$ for i = 1, 2 and all t.

$f_{0t}(x) = \begin{cases} r^{t-1}[40+8x] & x>0 \\ 0 & x=0 \end{cases}$ for all t.

Set 2: $f_{it}(x) = \begin{cases} r^{t-1}[3700+18x] & x>0 \\ 0 & x=0 \end{cases}$ for i = 1, 2 and all t.

$f_{0t}(x) = \begin{cases} r^{t-1}[4000+24x] & x>0 \\ 0 & x=0 \end{cases}$ for all t

where r is a discount factor.

Note that in each problem the cost functions are identical for dedicated technologies. In comparison with the first set of cost function, the second set of cost function has larger fixed charges in proportion to its variable cost. The two sets of cost functions are similar to those used in Luss (1979 and 1986).

(ii) Demand Patterns:

The basic module for generating product demands consists of two components, a base demand with linear growth and a random component. This may be described by the equation: $bt\xi_t$ where b is a growth parameter, t is a time periods, and ξ_t is a normally distributed random variable with a mean of 1.0 and a standard deviation of 0.1. (It may be noted that this provides a wide range of variation of ξ_t between 0.7 and 1.3.) To generate demands for the test problems, I considered two patterns of demand: independent and dependent.

(a) Independent demand:

In this case, the demand for each product in each period is generated randomly using the basic module described earlier. The demand for each product family grows following the pattern of $bt\xi_t$. b is set at 3 when the first set of cost functions is used, and is set at 50 when the second set of cost functions is used.

(b) Dependent demand:
      In this case, I use the basic module to generate the total demand of two product families (denoted as D_t, $D_t = bt\xi_t$). The demands of individual product families (denoted as d_{it}) are determined by generating P_{it}, the proportion of demand due to product i in period t (That is, $d_{it} = P_{it}D_t$). P_{1t} is generated as a random variable with a mean of μP_{1t} ($0 \leq \mu P_{1t} \leq 1$) and standard deviation of 0.1 and P_{2t} is equal to 1 - P_{1t}. If the random variable P_{1t} is greater than 1, then P_{1t} is equal to 1 and P_{2t} is equal to 0.
      In my test problems, b is set at 6 when the first set of cost function is used and b is 100 when the second set of cost functions is used. μP_{1t} is set at 0.5 and 0.7 sequentially. The dependent demand pattern, as a result, is more erratic than the independent demand pattern.

(iii) Length of the Planning Horizon:
      I consider a long term capacity planning with the horizon of 10.

(iv) Discount Factor:
      I assume 0.93 as discount factor.

      Thus I define six cases, with each case specified by the set of cost functions and the demand pattern (independent, dependent, etc.). For each case, I randomly generated ten problems, giving a total of 60 problems for this experiment. The heuristics were coded in FORTRAN and run on CDC Dual Cyber 170/150. Optimal solutions for the test problems are obtained through the MPSX mixed-integer programming package.
      Table 3.5 presents the summary computational results. In the table, for each case the following measures are provided: (i) number of times the solution provided by the heuristics was optimal; (ii) average relative error of heuristic solutions; (iii) maximum error of heuristic solutions; (iv) average deviation of heuristic solutions from lower bounds. Column "SP" in the table refers to the solution obtained by the application of the SP approach in the first stage, followed by the improvement heuristics. The results corresponding to the second approach appear in the "SMCP" column. Column "Better of Two" in the table refers to the solution obtained by comparing the SMCP and SP solutions. The results in the table are very encouraging and suggest that the heuristics perform very well. For example, in the case of the first set of cost functions and independent demand pattern (see row 1 in Table 1), while the average error of SMCP approach is 1.544%, that

of SP is 0.333%, the average error of the "Better of Two" solutions is only 0.326%.

The results above suggest that the solutions given by SP are superior to that given by SMCP. While this is true, I note the SP does not dominate SMCP. Also, the computational effort required by SP is more than that of SMCP. For example, average time for obtaining a solution using SMCP and SP respectively are 0.42 and 0.64 seconds. Both these methods require significantly shorter time compared with the 18.6 seconds for obtaining an optimal solution. It may be noted that the procedure to obtain optimal solutions is not suitable for general cost functions. Even for the cost functions considered in these experiments, the computational effort is likely to become prohibitive for larger problems.

It may be recalled that T_S, the planning horizon of SP, is a parameter that needs to be specified. In the test problems I experimented with five different values ranging from 5 to 9. These results suggest that the choice of T_S is not critical for my procedures. The initial solutions obtained with different values of T_S were of comparable quality. The differences were even lower after the application of the improvement heuristics.

I conclude this section with a brief discussion of the nature of expansion plans generated by the heuristics. It is interesting to note that even with deterministic demands, investments in the more expensive flexible technology are economical. For example, in my test problems, with the first cost set (corresponding to 40+8X and 30+7X), flexible capacity accounted on average for 28% of total capacity additions. In these examples, flexible capacity was typically 17% more expensive at the levels of investment suggested by the heuristic solution. Similarly, with the second cost set (corresponding to 4000+24X and 3700+18X), the flexible technology was viable even when it was 25% more expensive than dedicated technology. In these examples, flexible capacity accounted for 43% of total additions. Further, in the test problems, investments in flexible capacity increase as the demand patterns become more erratic, that is, change from independent to dependent patterns.

Another interesting point is that the investment in flexible technology in most test problems occurs early (usually in the first period) in the planning horizon. This suggests that flexible capacity acts primarily as a "cushion" to absorb the fluctuations in demand among products. The result of early investment in flexible capacity tends to minimize the total capacity additions. For example, with the use of flexible technology, total capacity additions may be limited to the maximal total demand in any period. In the absence of flexible capacity, the total capacity needed would be the sum of the highest demand for each product family.

3.6   SUMMARY AND EXTENSION

Thus far, I have studied a situation in which a firm has to develop an investment plan to satisfy the demands of its two-product families for a manufacturing system over a finite planning horizon. I have formulated the problem as a strategic investment planning model that can help the firm to decide the optimal mix of flexible and dedicated technologies with minimal total investment cost. By exploiting the special structure of the problem, I have developed two approaches to obtain an initial solution of the problem. Then I have developed heuristics to improve initial solutions. The computational results show that the heuristics perform well and that approximate optimal objective values are close to their lower bounds.

A natural extension of the investment model presented in this chapter is a provision for multiple-product families. While this is easy in principle, the formulation of **MCP** does not extend in an obvious manner, and subproblems of **SP** and **SMCP** types become intractable with increasing numbers of products. Another direction for extension of the model relates to issues of uncertainty in demand. This feature would be particularly attractive since flexible technologies are likely to have very significant impact in such scenarios. While some work has been reported in this context with linear costs and two-products, a number of issues, such as stochastic demands, multiple-product families, non-linear investment cost functions, etc., need to be examined in more detail.

IV. DYNAMIC CAPACITY EXPANSION PROBLEM WITH MULTIPLE PRODUCTS:TECHNOLOGY SELECTION AND TIMING OF CAPACITY ADDITIONS

Over the past decade, manufacturing flexibility has emerged as a competitive weapon and has contributed to a growing interest in modern technologies such as flexible manufacturing systems (FMS), computer integrated manufacturing (CIM), and flexible automation (FA). Recent developments in these technologies permit production of a wide variety of products with small changeover costs. Increased competition in the marketplace, particularly from overseas manufacturers, has resulted in short product cycles and has put a premium on flexibility in changing product mix in a dynamic fashion. Together, these factors encourage investment in facilities capable of producing several-product families. Modern technologies such as FMS and CIM are typically capital intensive, and capacity additions require substantial investments. The presence of economies of scale introduces additional complexity, thus making expansion decisions even more intricate.

A number of empirical studies indicate that while most managers have a good conceptual understanding of the benefits of modern technologies, methods for their evaluation and adoption are rather inadequate. For example, based on annual surveys of large manufacturers in North America, Europe, and Japan, Tombak and Meyer (1988), and Meyer et al. (1989) conclude that firms invest in flexible technology primarily for its ability to adapt to a wide variety of inputs and/or outputs. They also note that American firms are lagging behind in their efforts to overcome the tradeoffs between flexibility and cost efficiency. Meredith and Suresh (1986) observe that flexibility provided by advanced manufacturing systems is not captured by most economic justification methods used by firms, and that this has in turn led to the rejection of many worthwhile projects. In a series of related articles, Goldhar and Jelinek (1983, 1985) and Jelinek and Goldhar

(1983, 1984) examine the implications of flexible technologies for defining firms' long-term strategies. They use the term "economies of scope" to describe the ability to produce a wide variety of products. The authors note that the tradeoffs between economies of scale and of scope are little understood, and that investment and technology choice decisions are driven primarily by scale economies. These observations are consistent with those of Jaikumar (1986), who found that, in comparison with the Japanese, U.S. manufacturers installed fewer flexible systems. This is partly due to high costs of acquisition of flexible systems, and partly due to lack of appropriate evaluation methods.

I note that while some key issues related to the adoption of new technologies have been identified in the research described above, they do not provide a mechanism for evaluation of alternative technologies. Motivated by this need, I suggest a model-based approach to examine the tradeoffs between scale and scope economies. My objective is to develop tools to assist managers in making technology choices and investment decisions. More specifically, in this chapter I consider the technology choice and capacity expansion problem of a firm producing multiple products. Typically, flexible facilities are more expensive than dedicated facilities, and the trade-off is between increased flexibility to meet variations in product mix and higher investment cost. The objective is to minimize the total discounted investment cost to satisfy the product demands over a planning horizon (the problem is described in detail in Section 4.2.).

I observe that my model is suitable for long- and medium-term planning and can be applied in a variety of situations. For example, it may be used in the steel industry to determine the appropriate mix of mini and integrated steel plants. Other applications can be found in the fabrication, consumer electronics and automotive industries characterized by multiple products with relatively short life cycles and availability of alternative flexible technologies. Gerwin (1989) provided several cases describing the investment tradeoffs between flexible and dedicated technologies in the auto industry.

I use a finite-horizon, discrete-period model to capture the issues described above. Since the resulting problems are hard to solve optimally, I examine several heuristics to derive good investment strategies. In this development I draw extensively from the literature on capacity expansion and flexible manufacturing (see Section 4.1 for more details). My computational results suggest that the heuristics perform very well and require only a modest effort. They also illustrate the application of the methodology in examining the role of flexible technologies in a deterministic environment. Qualitatively, my results are consistent with the characteristics of flexible technologies described earlier. They also suggest that the optimal amount of flexible technology strongly depends on parameters related to scale economies, demand patterns, and relative costs of dedicated and modern technologies, and thus demonstrate a need for tools to support these strategic decisions.

The remainder of the chapter is organized as follows. In the following section I describe the capacity planning problem and provide a brief review of the related literature. Sections 4.2 and 4.3 are devoted respectively to the development of heuristics and lower bounds. I discuss the results of our computational experiments in Section 4.4. In Section 4.5, I conclude with a discussion of extensions of the approach to address related issues.

4.1 RELATED LITERATURE

Pioneering work in the area of capacity planning has been done by Manne (1961, 1967) who examined a single product case with linearly increasing demand over an infinite horizon and stationary costs (except for discounting). Extensions of Manne's model can be found in Srinivasan (1967), Erlenkotter (1967, 1977), and Manne and Veinott (1967). Freidenfelds (1980) and Whitt and Luss (1981) considered the case of uncertain demand. Lieberman (1989) used empirical tests to examine the hypotheses of the Manne and the Whitt and Luss models. The literature on variants of the problem with two-products can be found in Kalotay (1973), Erlenkotter (1974), Freidenfelds (1981), Merhaut (1975), Kalotay (1975), Wilson and Kalotay (1976), and Luss (1979, 1980). Extensions of the problem to more than two products have been explored in Luss (1983, 1986) and Lee and Luss (1987). For a comprehensive survey of the literature prior to 1982, the reader is referred to Luss (1982) and references therein.

Tradeoffs between scale economies and investment and transportation costs have been examined in the context of multiple-region capacity expansion problems. Manne (1967) and Erlenkotter (1967) examined the two-region, infinite-horizon problem for a single product with linearly increasing demand. Fong and Rao (1975) considered the finite horizon problem with nondecreasing demand and developed efficient algorithms based on a network representation of the problem. Fong and Srinivasan (1981a, 1981b, 1986) examined extensions of the problem to multiple regions and developed heuristic procedures. Klincewicz, Luss, and Yu (1988) described a multilocation model that combines location decisions (opening, closing and expansion) and assignment of demands to the facilities. We refer the reader to Karnani (1983) and Erlenkotter (1989) and references therein for details of facility location models that examine the tradeoffs between scale economies in production and transportation.

In recent years, there has been a growing body of literature focusing on the choice of technologies as a competitive weapon. For example, Hutchinson and Holland (1982) developed a simulation model to examine the tradeoff between flexible manufacturing systems (FMSs) and transfer lines (dedicated technology). Burstein (1986) developed a two-product model incorporating production decisions and choices between flexible and dedicated technology. Cohen and Halperin (1986) considered the optimal choice of a set of (fixed, variable) cost pairs of technologies in the single-product and dynamic-stochastic environment. Fine and Freund (1986) examined technology choices in a multi-product problem with static, stochastic demand patterns. Gupta et al. (1988) defined degree of flexibility as a critical parameter in technology selection and addressed related issues with two products.

While the foregoing discussion has focused on flexibility in product mix, we note that modern technologies provide flexibility in other dimensions such as volume, quality, routing and facility utilization. For example, Vander Veen and Jordan (1989) studied interaction between machine investment and utilization decisions involving part allocation and production cycles. Cohen and Moon (1989) studied the impact of scale economies and manufacturing complexity on supply chain facility networks. Tang (1989) examined capacity expansion and machine allocation decisions in a more detailed model of the production facility. Gaimon (1989) considered competition between two firms and examined its impact on new technology adoption and capacity addition. For a detailed description of research on economic evaluation models of manufacturing flexibility, the reader is referred to Fine (1989) and references therein.

The work reported in this chapter is similar in spirit to that of Fong and Rao (1975), Fong and Srinivasan (1981a, 1981b, 1986), and Luss (1986), but with important differences. First, I permit general demand patterns and do not require nondecreasing demands. Second, in my model, flexible technology provides complete product mix flexibility and can be used to produce some or all products with no conversion costs. As a result, a network representation similar to the one used by either Fong and Rao or Luss will not describe our capacity expansion problem. Third, I permit a more general class of dynamic concave cost functions. In contrast, the recent literature on technology choice is based on linear costs (and static demand patterns), while capacity expansion research focuses on fixed charge cost functions.

In principle, the Fong and Srinivasan model can be used describe the problem considered in this chapter by treating each product as a region, with transportation cost for dedicated (flexible) technologies set at infinity (zero). However, as noted earlier, this problem is difficult and the authors developed heuristics which do not extend to our problem in an obvious manner. As described later (Section 4.2.2), I do incorporate some of their ideas in my heuristic procedures.

4.2   THE CAPACITY EXPANSION PROBLEM (CP)

As mentioned earlier, I consider a firm producing multiple products in an environment characterized dynamic growth in market demand. The demand for each product family is assumed to be known over the planning horizon, and the objective is to determine a least-cost schedule of capacity additions to meet the product demands. The demand for each product family may be satisfied in the following manner: (i) by investments in facilities dedicated to producing items within the family (referred to as dedicated technology); (ii) by investments in facilities that are capable of producing several product families (referred to as flexible technology); (iii) by some combination of (i) and (ii). We also assume that both dedicated and flexible technologies exhibit significant economies of scale so that investments in plants with larger capacity are favored. Thus, I focus on the issues of choice of technology (dedicated versus flexible), time phasing, and size of capacity additions to minimize the total cost of meeting the demand for all products over the planning horizon.

In this section I discuss the development of heuristics to derive a good schedule of capacity additions to meet the forecast demand over the planning horizon. First, I present an algebraic formulation of the capacity expansion problem. In Section 4.2.1 I discuss heuristics for obtaining an initial solution for CP. In Section 4.2.2, I present improvement procedures. The following notation will be used to describe the problem:

Notation:

N: Number of product families

T: Number of time periods (represents the planning horizon of the problem)

i: index for product families and technology choices; technology of type i refers to dedicated technology capable of producing items in product i, $i = 1, 2,..., N$; $i = 0$ refers to flexible technology capable of producing all products

X_{it}: amount of capacity addition of type i in period t, i = 0,1,..., N; t = 1, 2,..., T

X_{i0}: initial capacity of type i

Y_{it}: amount of flexible capacity allocated to product family i in period t, i = 1, 2,..., N; t = 1, 2,..., T

d_{it}: demand for product family i in period t, i = 1, 2,..., N; t = 1, 2, ..., T

$f_{it} (\cdot)$: cost function for capacity type i in period t, i = 0,1,..., N; t = 1, 2,..., T

The capacity planning problem, CP is formulated as follows:

$$(CP) \quad Z_{CP} = \text{Min} \sum_{i=0}^{N} \sum_{t=1}^{T} f_{it}(X_{it})$$

Subject to:

$$\sum_{\tau=1}^{t} X_{it} + Y_{it} \geq d_{it} \qquad i = 1, 2,..., N; t = 1, 2,..., T \quad (1)$$

$$\sum_{i=1}^{N} Y_{it} \leq \sum_{\tau=0}^{t} X_{0\tau} \qquad\qquad t = 1, 2,..., T \quad (2)$$

$$X_{it} \geq 0 \qquad i = 0, 1,..., N; t = 1, 2,..., T \quad (3)$$

$$Y_{it} \geq 0 \qquad i = 1, 2,..., N; t = 1, 2,..., T \quad (4)$$

In the formulation above, the objective is to minimize the total discounted costs over the planning horizon. The discount factor is not explicit in the objective function, but it can be incorporated in the functions $f_{it} (\cdot)$. Observe that stationarity in costs is not necessary, and that the functions $f_{it} (\cdot)$ can be defined independently. This is a particularly useful feature in modeling new technologies, since advances in these areas could lead to cost reductions in the future. To reflect economies of scale, I assume that $f_{it} (\cdot)$ is concave. I observe that this is a characteristic found in many industries. Also, concavity of f_{it} permits inclusion of fixed costs. To simplify my presentation, I have not included variable operation costs in the objective function, but inclusion of these costs as linear functions of volume will not significantly affect my results and the procedures presented in this paper

(the implications of including the operating costs are discussed in Section 4.5.)

Constraints (1) specify that sufficient capacity should be allocated to satisfy the known demands for each product family in every period. I assume that the time periods are large (typically one year) and ignore inventory fluctuations. Constraints (2) ensure that the amount of flexible capacity used does not exceed its availability. Without loss of generality, I assume that initial capacity of dedicated technology is zero, i.e., $X_{i0} = 0$ for $i = 1, 2, \ldots, N$. If the initial capacities are non-zero, the demands d_{it} may be adjusted to be net of the initial capacity. This notion is similar to that of the concept of effective demand used in the context of hierarchical production planning (for example, see Hax and Candea (1984), p.408.). However, this simplification will not apply to flexible technology and I permit initial capacity X_{00} to take non-negative values.

The problem **CP** involves minimization of a concave objective function subject to linear constraints. It is well known that such a problem has an optimal solution at one of the extreme points. This property has been used in the development of procedures to obtain optimal or approximate optimal solutions to some capacity expansion problems. For example, Fong and Rao (1975), Luss (1979, 1980, 1986) and Lee and Luss (1987) used this property to solve a one-product, two-region problem, a two-product problem and a multi-product problem. However, it should be noted that even with the use of this property, it is difficult to develop efficient algorithms for deriving optimal solutions. Hence, I focus on heuristics to address the capacity expansion problem. In this development I make use of the results of Proposition 1, which permits restriction of expansion choices to integer values in cases when the product demands are integers.

Proposition 1: Consider the problem CP in which demands d_{it} are integral for $i = 1, 2, \ldots, N$; $t = 1, 2, \ldots, T$. There exists an optimal solution to CP in which capacity additions X_{it} take integral values. (please see Appendix F for a proof.)

4.2.1 HEURISTICS FOR CP (PHASE I)

In this section I propose a two-stage heuristic for obtaining an approximate solution to **CP**. In the first stage, the objective is to obtain a good initial solution by solving sequence of subproblems. In the second stage, several heuristics are used to improve upon the initial solution. My approach is similar to the one proposed by Fong and

Srinivasan (1986) for solving multi-region capacity expansion problems (MRDCEP). The subproblems for obtaining the initial solution for **CP** are quite different from those used in MRDCEP. My heuristics for deriving an initial solution may be described as a limited look-ahead procedure which involves solving sequences of subproblems with short planning horizons. Some of the heuristics in the second stage are similar to the ones used by Fong and Srinivasan. Before describing the heuristic, I first discuss a subproblem (**SP**) that forms the basis for deriving an initial solution to **CP**.

Limited Look-Ahead Procedure:

I define a subproblem (**SP**) that is similar in structure to **CP** with two important differences. First, the planning horizon of **SP** (denoted by T_S) is smaller than that of **CP**. Second, in **SP** I permit at most one investment in each type of technology. My objective in this approach is to define subproblems that yield good solutions with reasonable computational effort. However, I note that in spite of these simplifications, it is not easy to obtain an optimal solution to **SP**, and that I rely on heuristics to derive near-optimal solutions. I expect that with an appropriate choice of T_S, the restrictions on the number of capacity additions will not significantly affect the quality of the initial solution. This anticipation is based on the following observations:

(i) To derive an initial solution, I propose a rolling-horizon approach and solve a sequence of problems **SP**. As a result, only the first period results of **SP** are incorporated in the initial solution.

(ii) Intuition suggests that in problems with long horizons, investments in the first period are not seriously affected by demands in the later periods. This notion is supported by the results of the planning-horizon theorems obtained in the context of production planning (See Lundin and Morton (1975), p.714 and Hax and Candea (1984), p.76).

We observe that T_S may be a critical parameter in this approach. A low value of T_S may lead to solutions that will not capture the advantages of scale economies and result in frequent capacity additions. On the other hand, if T_S is too large, the restrictions on capacity additions are likely to result in fewer investments with correspondingly larger-sized plants. In Section 4.4, I examine empirically the impact of the choice of T_S on the quality of the solutions provided by the heuristics. I now present an algebraic formulation of **SP**.

Let X_0^{rj} denote a vector with T_s elements:

$$X_0^{rj} = \{(X_{01}, X_{02}, ..., X_{0r-1}, X_{0r}, X_{0r+1}, ..., X_{0Ts})\} \qquad (5)$$

with $X_{0t} = \begin{cases} 0 & \text{for } t = 1, 2, ..., T_s, t \ne r \\ j & \text{for } t = r \end{cases}$

Define χ to be the set of permissible investments in flexible technology (for the problem **SP**), i.e., $\chi = \{X_0^{rj} \ r = 1, 2, ..., T_s; 0 \le j \le U_{0r}\}$, where U_{0r} is the upper bound of X_{0r} (the magnitude of U_{0r} is described later in the initial solution procedure.

$$[\textbf{SP}] \qquad Z_{SP} = \min_{X_0^{rj} \in \chi} \ \sum_{t=1}^{T_s} f_{0t}(X_{0t}) + F(X_0^{rj})$$

$$= \min_{X_0^{rj} \in \chi} \ f_{0r}(j) + F(X_0^{rj}),$$

where $[\textbf{SPX}] \quad F(X_0^{rj}) = \min \sum_{t=1}^{T_s} \sum_{i=1}^{N} f_{it}(X_{it})$

subject to : (1), (2), (3) and (4) with T replaced by T_s.

It may be noted that the problem **SPX** is also not easy to solve, that is, even with the investments X_0^{rj} specified, it is not easy to determine optimal capacity additions in dedicated technologies. Hence, I propose to obtain an approximate solution by relaxing (2) into the objective and solving the dual problem $D(X_0^{rj})$ given by

$$D(X_0^{rj}) = \max_{\lambda \ge 0} \ \upsilon(X_0^{rj}, \lambda)$$

where $L(X_0^{rj}, \lambda): \ \upsilon(X_0^{rj}, \lambda)$

$$= \min \sum_{i=1}^{N} \sum_{t=1}^{T_s} f_{it}(X_{it}) + \sum_{t=1}^{T_s} \lambda_t \left(\sum_{i=1}^{N} Y_{it} - \sum_{\tau=0}^{t} X_{0\tau} \right)$$

subject to : (1), (3) and (4) with T replaced by T_s.

Note that given X_0^{rj} and λ, $L(X_0^{rj}, \lambda)$ decomposes into N problems that can be solved relatively easily. Also, $\upsilon(X_0^{rj}, \lambda)$ provides a lower bound for the objective value of $F(X_0^{rj})$ in [SPX], and the best lower bound is given by $D(X_0^{rj})$, i.e., $\upsilon(X_0^{rj}, \lambda) \leq D(X_0^{rj}) \leq F(X_0^{rj})$. Furthermore, a feasible solution to **SP X** can be constructed rather easily from the solution to $L(X_0^{rj}, \lambda)$. I propose to obtain an approximate solution to **SP** by implicitly considering all possible values for vector X_0^{rj}, and by solving the corresponding problems **SPX**.

The flow chart in Figure 4.2.1 describes a heuristic based on the foregoing discussion for obtaining an initial solution to **CP**. As indicated in this procedure, it is necessary to solve a number of **SPX** to obtain a solution for each **SP**. An upper bound on the number of subproblems is given by $T_s(U_{max} + 1)$. However, in the implementation of the heuristic, I reduced the number of subproblems by computing a crude lower bound for $F(X_0^{rj})$. In this procedure, given investments in flexible technology in period r, I identify the total investment required before and after period r to satisfy the product demands. A lower bound is computed by assuming all investment before period r occurs in period r-1, and all investment after period r occurs in period t_e. By incorporating this procedure, I was able to reduce the number of subproblems by about 30%.

4.2.2   IMPROVEMENT HEURISTICS (PHASE 2)

In this section I present heuristics to improve upon the feasible solution obtained by the methods of section 4.2.1. In most of these heuristics, I examine effects of changes in capacity additions during appropriately defined short intervals. The procedures are myopic in the sense that only changes leading to cost reductions are adopted and that the schedule of capacity additions is changed accordingly. These changes, classified as (i) Temporal Shift and (ii) Technology Shift, are described briefly below (the details are presented in Appendix D):

(i) Temporal Shift: I consider one type of technology at a time, and assume that all investments in other technologies are fixed. Two alternatives to adjust the expansion plans are examined: (a) Global Shift and (b) Forward/Backward Shift. In Global Shift, I derive an optimal expansion plan for each technology by assuming that expansion plans for other technologies are fixed. In Forward/Backward Shifts, I examine changes in expansion plans within intervals defined by successive

capacity additions in the same type of technology in chronological and reverse sequences.

(ii) Technology Shift: In these procedures, I examine the effect of adjustments in capacity additions among technologies. I consider two cases: Period Shift and Interval Shift. Period Shift focuses on changes in the mix of capacity additions in one period. With Interval Shift I examine changes in technology mix as well as timing of capacity additions during suitably chosen subintervals.

Though some of the shifts mentioned above are developed from Fong and Srinivasan's improvement heuristics, my procedures are more involved since the total amount of capacity additions is not a constant and depends on the amount of flexible capacity. It may be noted that the heuristics described above represent alternative methods to generate incremental changes in the schedule of capacity additions, and may be implemented in several ways. Also, it is not necessary to incorporate all of them in the second phase of the algorithm. Figure 4.2.2 describes my implementation for the numerical examples described in Section 4. In this scheme, I alternatively examine temporal and technology shifts until no further improvement is possible. Figure 4.2.2 provides a general process sequence: (i) Temporal Shift with only Forward & Backward Shift; (ii) Technology Shift with both Period and Interval Shifts; and (iii) Temporal Shift with only Global Shift. In the computational experiments of Section 4.4, I found that two iterations were required in most test problems.

4.3 LOWER BOUNDS AND OPTIMAL SOLUTIONS TO CP

In this section I discuss procedures to compute lower bounds on the value of the objective function to CP. My aim in this analysis is to present methods that can be used to establish the quality of the solutions provided by the heuristics of Section 4.2. In addition, I also present an integer programming formulation of CP (ICP) that may be used to determine an optimal solution to CP for small problems.

4.3.1 AGGREGATE LOWER BOUND (ALB)

This is a simple procedure that provides a method to compute a lower bound on Z_{CP}. The method relies on deriving a cost function for each period that is a lower envelope of the functions $f_{it}(\cdot)$. With this cost function and a demand vector that represents the total demand for all products, a lower bound on Z_{CP} is obtained by solving a one-product problem similar to the one solved by Manne and Veinott (1967). This problem is equivalent to the one examined by Wagner and Whitin (1958), and can be solved by the dynamic programming procedures of $O(T^2)$.

While the lower-bounding procedure described above is easy to compute, the quality of the bound depends on the closeness of the functions $f_{it}(\cdot)$ to the lower envelope. In particular, I expect the lower bound to be poor when: (a) flexible technology is significantly more expensive than dedicated facilities; (b) the demand patterns are so erratic that considerable amounts of flexible technology investments are optimal; (c) significant scale economies are present.

4.3.2   *DUAL LOWER BOUND (DLB)*

The second procedure I describe relies on Lagrangian relaxation of CP in which constraint (2) is relaxed, and I solve the corresponding dual to obtain the best lower bound. Note that the relaxed problem decomposes into N+1 subproblems. However, the bounding procedure is not straightforward, since the subproblem corresponding to flexible technology does not give a meaningful bound. Hence I propose to determine a lower bound by keeping the total amount of capacity in flexible technology fixed. A lower bound to CP is then obtained by considering all levels of investment in flexible technology. In deriving this lower bound I consider the following two methods:

Availability Method (AM):
In this method, a lower bound on the cost of investments in dedicated technologies is found by assuming that all flexible capacity is available in the first period. Similarly, a lower bound on the cost of flexible technology is found by assuming that the required dedicated technology capacities are available in the first period. Let F_0 be the total amount of investment in the flexible technology. Then constraint (2) in CP becomes

$$\sum_{i=1}^{N} Y_{it} \leq F_0 + X_{00} \qquad t = 1, 2, ..., T \qquad (6)$$

where X_{00} is the initial capacity of the flexible technology which is a constant.

The following model gives the lower bound to CP for given F_0:

$$LB(F_0) = D1(F_0) + D2(F_0)$$

where $D1(F_0)$ is the corresponding dual in which (6) is relaxed. This is similar to $D(X_0^{rj})$ described in Section 4.2.1, and

$$D2(F_0) = \min \sum_{t=1}^{T} f_{0t}(X_{0t})$$

s.t.

$$\sum_{\tau=1}^{t} X_{0\tau} \geq d'_t \text{ and } X_{0t} \geq 0 \qquad t = 1, 2, ..., T$$

where d'_t can be considered as the minimum demand for flexible technology in period t, i.e., $d'_t = \max\{0, \sum_{i=1}^{N} d_{it} - (d_{max} - F_0)\}$ for t = 1, 2,..., T. (d_{max} is the maximal total demand among all the periods, i.e., $d_{max} = \max_{1 \leq t \leq T} \{ \sum_{i=1}^{N} d_{it} \}$.)

Adding Constraint Method (ACM):

In this method, we add an additional constraint to CP, that is, $\sum_{t=1}^{T} X_{0t} = F_0$ where F_0 is the given total amount of capacity of flexible technology. We relax constraint (2) and solve N+1 subproblems to obtain a lower bound for **CP**. The maximum of the Lagrangian solutions gives the best lower bound to CP for the given amount of total capacity in flexible technology.

Figure 4.3.2 summarizes the discussion above and presents a procedure for computing a lower bound on Z_{CP}. We observe that the bounds obtained by the AM are tight for extreme values of F_0: 0 and d_{max}. This follows from the fact that, when F_0 is zero, $D1(F_0)$ will be equal to the cost of an optimal investment plan. Likewise, when the investment in flexible technology is d_{max}, no other investment is necessary and $D2(F_0)$ will be equal to the corresponding optimal cost. Hence, we expect the lower bounds given by this method to be good for low and high values of F_0. The quality of the bounds is likely to deteriorate for intermediate values of F_0. We expect that the ACM which does not involve assumptions regarding timing of capacity additions will provide better bounds for intermediate values of F_0. These conclusions are supported by the results of computational experiments of Section 4.4.

4.3.3 AN INTEGER PROGRAMMING FORMULATION OF CP (ICP)

In this section, I present an integer programming formulation of the capacity planning problem. In this formulation, I use the following additional notation:

j: index for amount of capacity addition (assumed to be integers)

C_{ijt}: cost of adding j units of capacity of technology i in period t, $i = 0, 1,..., N$; $t = 1, 2,..., T$

$xmax_i$: maximal amount of investment that can be made for technology i, $i = 0, 1,..., N$.

X_{00}: initial amount of capacity in flexible technology which is a constant

$$\delta_{ijt} = \begin{cases} 1 & \text{if } j \text{ units of technology } i \text{ invested at period } t \\ 0 & \text{otherwise} \end{cases}$$

$$[\text{ICP}] \quad \min: \quad \sum_{i=0}^{N} \sum_{j=1}^{xmax_i} \sum_{t=1}^{T} C_{ijt}\, \delta_{ijt}$$

subject to:

$$\sum_{j=1}^{xmax_i} \sum_{\tau=1}^{t} \delta_{ij\tau}\, j + \quad Y_{it} \geq d_{it}$$

$$i = 1, 2,..., N; t = 1, 2,..., T$$

$$- \sum_{j=1}^{xmax_0} \sum_{\tau=1}^{t} \delta_{0j\tau}\, j + \sum_{i=1}^{N} Y_{it} \leq X_{00} \qquad t = 1, 2,..., T$$

$$\sum_{j=0}^{xmax_i} \delta_{ijt} \quad = 1$$

$$i = 1, 2,..., N; t = 1, 2,..., T$$

$$Y_{it} \geq 0$$

$$i = 1, 2,..., N; \ t = 1, 2,..., T$$

$$\delta_{ijt} = \{1, 0\}$$

$$i = 1, 2,..., N; \ j = 0, 1,..., xmax_i; \ t = 1, 2,..., T$$

where $xmax_i = \max_{1 \leq t \leq T} \{d_{it}\}$ for $i = 1, 2,..., N$;

$$xmax_0 = \max_{1 \leq t \leq T} \{\sum_{i=1}^{N} d_{it}\}.$$

Following the results of Proposition 1, it is clear that an optimal solution to **ICP** is also optimal to **CP**. However, it may be noted that ICP involves large number of integer variables. As a result, it will be very difficult to obtain optimal solutions even for moderate-sized problems. In the computational experiments reported in Section 4.4, I use this procedure to compute optimal solution for test problems in order to evaluate the quality of the solution provided by the heuristics.

4.4 COMPUTATIONAL RESULTS

The objective of the computational experiments reported in this section is two-fold. First, I wanted to examine the quality of the heuristics by comparing the approximate solution with the optimal in a series of small test problems. In these experiments, optimal solutions were obtained by solving the corresponding ICP (see Section 4.3.3) using the MPSX package. Second, I illustrate the application of the heuristics in examining the role of flexible technology under a variety of conditions. Thus we generated larger sized test problems that are more representative of practical situations.

In the design of the test problems we considered a number of factors: cost functions, demand patterns, number of products, number of time periods, and discount factors. A total of 360 test problems were generated. Table 4.1 describes these factors in detail. While most are self explanatory, the choice of cost function and demand pattern require some elaboration. I tested the heuristics on two types of cost functions that are commonly found in the industry: power (Cobb Douglas) and fixed charge functions. The parameters were selected so as to provide a wide range of cost differential between dedicated and flexible technologies. In generating product demands, I considered two types of demand pattern: independent and dependent. In the former case, demand for each product is independent of other products. The basic module for generating demands consists of two components: a base demand with linear growth, and a multiplicative random term. This procedure, described in detail in Table 4.1, results in relatively wide variations in demand. For the case of dependent demands, aggregate demand is generated using the same scheme. The demands for individual products are determined by randomly generating the proportions of demands (described in Table 4.1).

For the sake of brevity, I present only the summary results, and do not include the problem data and the details of the solution. I now describe the results in detail.

4.4.1 DISCUSSION OF RESULTS

The quality of the heuristic solutions was examined in a series of tests with problems that had a limited and specific scope. The summary results presented in Tables 4.4.1a and 4.4.1b are very encouraging. The approximate solutions were optimal for 120 of 160 test problems. Even in the cases when the solutions were not optimal, average relative errors were very small (.07% - .63%), with a maximum relative error of 1.83%. The tables also indicate the quality of the lower bounds. It is not surprising to see that ALB does not perform well and in some cases it is 25% below the optimal. The DLB, which requires more work, provides more consistent results, with deviations in the range of 5% to 12% from the optimal.

In the remainder of the test problem I illustrate the application of the heuristics to examine the role of flexible technologies in a variety of situations. (Since it was not possible to obtain optimal solutions in these cases, I compare the heuristic solutions with the ALB.) Summary results presented in Tables 4.4.1c, 4.4.1d, and 4.4.1e highlight several interesting results that are briefly described below:

(i) Substantial investments in flexible technology are economically justified even when they are significantly more expensive than dedicated technologies. Not surprisingly, as the cost of flexible technology increases, the amount of investment decreases.

(ii) Investments in flexible technology increase as the demand pattern becomes more erratic. In other words, the dependent demand patterns require more investment in flexible technology.

(iii) Investments in flexible technology increase with increasing scale economies. This suggests that there is no inherent incompatibility between scale and scope economies, and is in contrast to the observations that cite scale economies lead to larger investments in dedicated technologies (see Jelinek and Goldhar (1983, 1984).

(iv) Investments in flexible technology occur early in the planning horizon. This suggests that flexible capacity acts primarily as a "cushion" to absorb the fluctuations in demand among products. Further, the amount of flexible capacity (relative to the total) is not significantly affected by the number of product families.

(v) The average deviations of the heuristic solution to the ALB are consistent with those observed in the first set of test problems. This suggests that quality of the heuristics may not deteriorate with the problem size.

4.4.2 RELATED COMMENTS

It may be recalled that the planning horizon, T_S, of the subproblems SP was a parameter to be specified for deriving an initial solution. In the test problems, we experimented with several values of T_S. The results suggest that T_S is not a critical parameter. The quality of the initial solutions were comparable with alternate values of T_S, with no one choice dominating the others. The differences were even lower after the application of the improvement heuristics in phase 2.

The first phase of the heuristic procedures provided consistently good initial solutions, thus justifying the somewhat elaborate procedures in this phase. As a result, the scope for improvement in the second phase was rather limited. However, in the few instances that the initial solution was not very good, the second phase procedures produced rapid improvements.

Although computational time is not a critical issue in this research, for the sake of completeness I provide some details of the computational effort required. The heuristic algorithms were coded in Fortran and run on CDC Dual Cyber 170/175. The optimal solutions were obtained by solving the MPSX software on IBM 3081. The heuristic solution for small-sized test problems required about 7 seconds. For other problems (larger demands), the average time increased to 13 seconds. In the ten period problems, the average computation time was 30 seconds. In contrast, the computation time with the MPSX system varied from 14 seconds to 6.3 minutes. I note that for larger problems, in general, it is not possible to obtain an optimal solution using this procedure.

4.5   CONCLUSION

In this chapter I have considered the problem of capacity expansion and investment planning in an environment characterized by multiple products and dynamic demands. My objective was to develop tools to help managers examine choices in technology, together with sizing and timing of capacity additions. In particular, my focus was on the tradeoff between flexible and dedicated technologies. I developed heuristics to provide good solutions with reasonable effort. We also present procedures to compute lower bounds on the optimal solution. My computational results suggest that the procedures perform well and provide acceptable solutions. Thus my methodology can be used to examine the economic viability of alternative technologies in a dynamic environment.

For the sake of simplicity in presentation, I have not included operating costs and costs of idle capacity. The model can be modified to incorporate these aspects. If these costs are linear, the solution procedures will extend in a straightforward manner. In addition to incorporation of these costs, a number of issues remain to be studied. Since modern technologies are capable of producing a variety of products, an obvious and important direction of extension is to provide for several alternative technologies with varying degrees of flexibility. My model can be modified to incorporate this issue by specifying the subset of products that can be produced by each type of technology. Although the solution procedures may be more complex, the decomposition methods developed in this chapter can be extended to handle this issue of manufacturing flexibility.

As well, I note that increased flexibility is consonant with risk avoidance and has potentially more impact (and benefits) in environments characterized by uncertainty. The models presented in this chapter are primarily deterministic in nature and do not consider these factors. Therefore, the work in this chapter needs to be extended in several directions that will address uncertainty. An important issue is the development of capacity expansion models with multiple products and dynamic uncertain demands. Though the case of static uncertain demands has been examined by several researchers, further analysis and a more extensive study of dynamic uncertain demands is needed to support the economic evaluation of flexible technologies. Uncertainty in acquisition costs and the complexity of new technologies are other issues that are important in this context. Another interesting problem with strategic implications relates to the integration of technology and expansion choices with marketing decisions. In such scenarios the objective is to choose demand and price levels, and the appropriate mix of production technologies. Hence, extensions which incorporate these factors will result in a comprehensive model that permits simultaneous evaluation of several key elements.

V. TECHNOLOGY CHOICE WITH STOCHASTIC DEMANDS AND DYNAMIC CAPACITY ALLOCATION: A TWO-PRODUCT ANALYSIS

In recent years, technology choice has become particularly important to operations managers as a result of developments in new, flexible technologies that provide a variety of benefits that include manufacturing flexibility, zero set-up cost, reduction of inventory and quality improvements. Among these, product mix flexibility is an important characteristic that permits production of a range of products without costly setup, and enables quick and efficient introduction of new products. Many modern technologies such as Computer Aided Design (CAD), Computer Aided Manufacturing (CAM), Computer Aided Engineering (CAE), and Computer Integrated Manufacturing (CIM) have such capability. In today's dynamic environment, manufacturing flexibility has become a competitive weapon for managers to cope with changing product mix and with uncertainties in demand.

While these modern technologies provide great operational flexibility, they are expensive to acquire in comparison to dedicated technologies with specialized equipment designed to produce a limited range of products more efficiently. The problem is further complicated by the presence of scale economies in capacity addition. One of the key decisions in this environment relates to choice of appropriate technology by considering the tradeoff between scale and scope economies.

In this chapter, I consider issues related to technology choice and expansion decisions in an environment characterized by uncertain demands. My objective is two-fold: (i) to provide a model-based approach to address tradeoffs between flexible and dedicated technologies in the presence of scale economies, and (ii) to develop an effective method of obtaining an approximate solution for the resulting model in order to determine the appropriate technology mix. I believe my results provide a link between two streams of literature dealing with capacity expansion and evaluation of flexible technologies, and complement current research on the subject. I recognize that besides economies of scope, flexible technologies provide other advantages not explicitly included in my model. Thus the model results should be used in conjunction with these potential benefits in making technology and capacity decisions. In this context, the model presented in this chapter may be interpreted as a building block in the development of a comprehensive framework for technology and capacity choices.

Specifically, in this paper I consider a two-product environment with stationary, stochastic demands. The objective is to determine the optimal mix of technologies and capacities necessary to satisfy specified service levels. I permit concave cost functions to reflect scale economies, and develop a non-linear program to capture the key issues in the problem. The resulting model is fairly general, but intractable for deriving analytical results. Hence I focus on computational methods to describe the related tradeoffs and, present a detailed analysis of a special case with uniform distributions to illustrate my solution approach.

My choice of the two-product case is motivated by two factors. First, a number of studies reported in the literature indicate wide applications for two-product models. Second, the two-product case is more tractable and can be considered as a building block for developing more general models. Also, each product could represent a family of items with similar manufacturing characteristics. This type of aggregation is common in hierarchical approaches to capacity and production planning (for example, see Hax and Meal (1975), and Hax and Candea (1984)). Thus, a two-product model could reasonably approximate facilities producing several similar products. In the remainder of this chapter, the terms of product and product family are used synonymously with the understanding that a product family represents a collection of similar items or products. Similarly, the multi-period, static demand case with one investment opportunity is appropriate for medium-term planning (a 1-2 year planning horizon with monthly time periods is not uncommon.) Again, the model can be considered as a building block for the development of multi-product and/or multi-period stochastic models.

This chapter is organized as follows. In the next section, I discuss some key factors and review the related literature. Following this, in Section 2 I describe the capacity planning problem and present a stochastic investment model. Section 3 deals with the analysis of a subproblem that forms the basis for my solution procedure described in Section 4. I present some illustrative examples in Section 5 and conclude in Section 6 with a discussion of extensions of my model.

5.1 PROBLEM MOTIVATION AND RELATED RESEARCH

The problem of capacity expansion and technology selection is complex and depends on a number of environmental factors. To examine related issues, a variety of approaches have been adopted in the economics, management science and operations research literature. A comprehensive review of prior work is beyond the scope of this study. Instead, in this section, I discuss some key factors and briefly describe the related literature in order to provide a proper focus for the work presented in this chapter.

Much of the initial work in the capacity planning literature focused on deterministic environments with dynamic demands in the presence of scale economies in investment. For example, Kalotay (1973), Erlenkotter (1974), and Luss (1979, 1980) examined variants of the two-product problem with technology choices characterized by limited flexibility. More recently Luss (1986), and Lee and Luss (1987) explored extensions of the problem to multiple products. For a detailed discussion of related issues in this environment I refer the reader to Luss (1982) and Li and Tirupati (1992), and references therein.

It is important to note that recent developments in modern technologies such as CIM and FMS provide a range of benefits that are not adequately captured in the deterministic capacity expansion models described above. These benefits include improved quality, customization and operational flexibility on several dimensions--routing, volume, and product mix. For detailed discussions of these and other aspects of flexibility, I refer the reader to Noori (1987) and Sethi and Sethi (1990), who suggest that these technologies are suitable for large-variety, medium-volume production. In this chapter, I focus on product mix flexibility--the ability to produce a range of products with little or no setup or conversion costs. This feature has also been referred to as production flexibility and scope economies.

The motivation for the work described in this chapter comes from empirical studies reported in Jaikumar (1986), Goldhar and Jelinek (1983, 1985), Jelinek and Goldhar (1983, 1984), Tombak and Meyer (1988), and Meyer et al. (1989). These studies indicate that lack of adequate evaluation methods is one of the primary reasons for slow adoption of modern flexible technologies by American manufacturers in comparison with those in Japan and Europe. They also identify that scale economies are present and, in most cases, play a significant role in investment decisions. In contrast, scope economies are not directly incorporated in evaluation methodologies. Similar findings have led Kaplan (1986) to characterize investment decisions in flexible technologies as "justification by faith". I also note that presence of scale economies has been known for a long time. For example, Manne (1967) provides several examples from the fertilizer, petrochemical, cement, and other process industries. In contrast to this empirical evidence, most of the modeling literature dealing with technology evaluation assumes linear or convex costs. Work reported by Bird (1987), Fine and Freund (1990), and Gupta et al. (1988) is representative of this stream of research. (Cohen and Halperin (1986) is an exception and provides for fixed costs. However, this work deals with single products and does not explicitly show capacity decisions.) It maybe noted that these assumptions (linearity or convexity) result in tractable models and provide some insights. However, it is not clear if the results extend to cases with scale economies. Hence, in this chapter, I focus on concave cost functions that capture several types of scale economies.

Modeling of demand behavior is a major factor that determines the complexity of the resulting decision models. As mentioned earlier, a substantial amount of work dealing with deterministic demands has been reported in the literature. However, the benefits of operational flexibility are considerably enhanced in the presence of uncertainties, and hence this factor is addressed explicitly in recent literature dealing with evaluation of flexibility. For example, Hutchinson and Holland (1982) and Cohen Halperin (1986) present models to discuss related issues with single product, while Bird (1987), Fine and Freund (1990a), and Gupta (1990) focus on multiple products. Typically, the objective function in these models includes shortage costs in addition to investment and operating costs. Alternatively, if product prices are known, the problem may be formulated with a profit maximizing objective function. It may be noted that in these models, in addition to investment decisions, it is necessary to determine production levels as well.

While the above approach is attractive in principle, the difficulties in estimating shortage costs are well known and often management-specified service levels are used as surrogates. In inventory management and production planning literature it is recognized that in many instances, service level measures obviate the need to estimate shortage costs, and are more acceptable and facilitate implementation. (However, it is true that corresponding to each service level, it is possible to determine an implied shortage cost.) In this chapter, my focus on service level as a performance measure is motivated by two observations: (i) the literature on the subject is somewhat sparse (as described later, Chakravarty (1989) is an exception), and (ii) this measure figures rather prominently in the empirical studies cited earlier.

Manufacturing flexibility coupled with demand uncertainty gives rise to allocation problems that have implications for capacity decisions. The nature of the production environment dictates the modeling choices in this context, and two approaches have been described in the literature. In the simpler approach, allocation of flexible capacity to product families is required before demand realizations are observed. This model is somewhat restrictive, but appropriate in situations with limited flexibility. In the second approach, which is suitable for situations with complete product mix flexibility, allocations of flexible capacity are made after demands are realized. The latter model captures, to a large extent, the dynamics associated with these modern, flexible technologies. I also note that in the latter case, when the total demand exceeds available capacity, additional complications are introduced because of choices in allocation of flexible capacity among products. The reader will recognize that in such situations a variety of allocation schemes, commonly termed rationing policies, are possible. While some results have been developed for specific rationing policies (for example, see Chakravarty (1989)), the literature on this issue is rather sparse.

I note that the literature on the subject of technology choice and capacity planning is rather diverse and related work has been reported, among others, by Fine and Freund (1989), Chakravarty (1986), and Andreou (1990). I refer the reader to a survey article by Fine (1990) and Gupta and Buzacott (1991) for a detailed discussion of economic evaluation of manufacturing flexibility.

In summary, the foregoing discussion provides the motivation the factors considered in this chapter. These include (a) scale economies in investment, (b) specified service levels, (c) uncertain demands, and (d) incorporation of the effect of rationing policies. It may be noted that my problem is similar to that of Chakravarty (1989) in two respects. First, in both problems uncertainties in demand are addressed by specifying service level objectives. (However, the measures are not identical.) Second, the detailed analysis presented in this chapter is also based on independent uniform distribution for product demand. However, there are significant differences between our work and the earlier literature. First, our model permits general concave investment cost functions to capture economies of scale. This is in contrast to the linear costs assumed in Chakravarty's model and in earlier research. This important feature results in concave minimization problems that are not easy to solve. Second, in addition to service level for individual products, I permit specification of service levels for groups of product families. While this may result in some redundancy, it does provide additional flexibility to managers in formulating demand and service objectives. Third, my model does not require specification of rationing policies and guarantees meeting service objectives independent of such policies. While my model results in higher levels of investment and improved service levels, the model is quite useful since rationing policies are operational decisions and a variety of schemes are possible. At the planning stage, prescribing a policy may be unnecessarily restrictive and misleading.

Before describing the model in detail, I conclude this section with some additional remarks about the problem considered in this chapter. First, the two-product model is motivated partly by application and partly by tractability considerations. A number of studies reported in the literature are based on applications with two-product families. For example, Kalotay (1973), Luss (1979, 1980), and Burstein (1986) examined two-product technology choice problems in manufacturing, communication, and flexible manufacturing systems. Second, the assumption of stationarity in demands is somewhat restrictive, but still has potential for applications. For example, this may be reasonable for medium-term planning. In such cases, the number of opportunities for investment is limited and capacity choices are made at the beginning of the planning horizon. However, resource allocation decisions (the assignment of flexible capacity to products) are dynamic and may be made in every period following demand realizations. I refer the reader to Fine and Freund (1990b) for a discussion of other related applications with stationary, stochastic demands.

5.2 AN INVESTMENT MODEL FOR TECHNOLOGY CHOICE PROBLEMS WITH TWO-PRODUCTS FAMILIES

In this chapter, I consider a technology choice problem faced by a firm manufacturing a number of products grouped into two-product families. I assume that the demand for each product family is a random variable. In order to provide a reasonable service to customers, the firm prescribes service levels for individual product families. The service levels are specified as probability of satisfying all demand for the product in any given period. This may also be interpreted as the fraction of time that the demands are satisfied. In addition, I permit specification of joint service level which requires that all demand (for both products) be satisfied with the specified probabilities.

The investment planning problem examined in this chapter deals with the choice of technology and additions of capacity to satisfy the prescribed service levels. I assume that the product demands may be satisfied by (i) dedicated plants designed to produce one product family, (ii) plants with flexible technology, or (iii) a combination of (i) and (ii). Further, I assume that there is only one opportunity for investment which is made at the beginning of a planning horizon. The objective is to minimize the total investment cost in both flexible and dedicated plants.

For the sake of simplicity, I assume that the variable production costs for each family do not depend on the type of technology used, and omit these costs from the model. However, this is not a serious limitation and the model can be modified to incorporate these aspects. I also assume that there are no salvage costs at the end of planning horizon.

Additionally, I make the following assumptions:

(i) demands for the two-product families follow independent but not necessarily identical distributions
(ii) investment cost functions are concave to reflect economies of scale

The following notation is used to describe the problem:

Notation:
T: planning horizon
i: index for product families and technology choices; technology of type i refers to dedicated technology capable of producing items in product family i, $i = 1, 2$; $i = 0$ refers to flexible technology capable of producing all products.
d_{it}: demand for product i in period t (random variable), $i = 1, 2$; $t = 1, 2, ..., T$
S_i: prescribed service level for product family i, $i = 1, 2$
S_{12}: prescribed service level for joint product family 1 and 2
X_i: amount of capacity addition in technology i, $i = 0, 1, 2$
$f_i(\cdot)$: investment cost function for technology i, $i = 0, 1, 2$

The resulting model, called the two-product capacity-technology model (TPCT), is as follows:

$$\text{(TPCT)} \quad Z_{TPCT} = \text{Min:} \sum_{i=0}^{2} f_i(X_i)$$

subject to:

$$P(d_{it} \le X_i) + P(X_i \le d_{it} \le X_i + X_0, \sum_{j=1}^{2} d_{jt} \le \sum_{j=0}^{2} X_j) \ge S_i$$

$$i = 1, 2; \ t = 1, 2, ..., T \quad (1)$$

$$P(d_{1t} \le X_1 + X_0, \ d_{2t} \le X_2 + X_0, \sum_{i=1}^{2} d_{it} \le \sum_{i=0}^{2} X_i) \ge S_{12}$$

$$t = 1, 2, ..., T \quad (2)$$

$$X_i \ge 0 \quad i = 0, 1, 2 \quad (3)$$

In this model, constraints (1) guarantee satisfaction of service level for product family i. It may be noted that the service level for each product family (left-hand side of (1)) may be computed as the sum of two terms. The first term corresponds to the case when demand for product i is less than its dedicated capacity (X_i) and hence trivially satisfied. The second term describes the case when demand is larger than X_i. In this instance, the demands for the two products are such that the available flexible capacity (X_0) together with dedicated capacity is sufficient to meet the demand for product i without any need for rationing. Observe that in this instance it is possible to have shortages in one product while satisfying the demand for the other. Similarly, constraint (2) guarantees the satisfaction of joint service level, which is expressed as the probability that demand for each product family is less than the sum of dedicated and flexible capacities and that total demand is less than total available capacity. (These constraints are discussed in more detail in Section 3.) Constraints (3) denote non-negativity requirement.

5.3   ANALYSIS OF TPCT(X_0), A SUBPROBLEM RELATED TO TPCT

Clearly, TPCT is a difficult problem for which it is not easy to obtain optimal solutions. First, the objective function is concave. Second, the set of feasible solutions, in general, do not form a convex set. Thus application of standard procedures is not adequate to derive optimal solutions. It may be noted that restrictions on limiting capacity additions to the first period and stationarity of demand distributions permit some simplification. Thus, it is sufficient to consider a one-period version of TPCT. In spite of this simplification the problem remains difficult. In this section I analyze in detail a subproblem derived from TPCT that forms the basis for a solution procedure described in Section 5.4. The subproblem, denoted as TPCT(X_0) is a restricted version of the single-period TPCT in which the amount of flexible technology is specified and the objective is to determine an optimal mix of dedicated technology capacities. To make my analysis specific and to illustrate my approach, I make the following additional assumptions in the remainder of the paper:

(a) investment cost functions include a fixed charge to reflect scale economies and have the following forms:

$$f_i(x) = \left\{ \begin{array}{ll} 0 & \text{if } x = 0 \\ F_i + C_i x & \text{if } x > 0 \end{array} \right. \quad i = 0, 1, 2$$

(b) demands follow uniform distributions $(0 - \beta_i, i = 1, 2)$

I note that assumption (a) is not critical to my approach and is primarily intended for simplifying the presentation. The analysis and the results extend, with minor modifications, to other concave cost functions. As a consequence of assumption (b), feasible solutions of the subproblem form a convex set. Thus, this assumption is somewhat critical and results in considerable simplification. (However, the lower limit of 0 for the demand distributions are not crucial and are made to simplify the presentation.) I conjecture that this result may extend to other well-behaved probability distributions such as normal distributions, provided that service levels are reasonably high (which is not uncommon in practice). However, I note that this result is not true in general, and that it is easy to construct examples in which the feasible region of the subproblem does not form a convex set. I now present the details.

The subproblem TPCT(X_0) is derived by considering a single period version of TPCT in which investment in flexible technology, X_0 is specified. In this formulation, I express the service level constraints in terms of decision variables X_i, and demands d_{it} do not appear. Hence, the multi-period TPCT is equivalent to a single-period problem. TPCT(X_0) with uniform distributions may be described algebraically as follows:

$$[\text{TPCT}(X_0)] \ F(X_0) \ = \min: \ \sum_{i=1}^{2} f_i \, (X_i)$$

subject to:

$$X_i + \frac{X_0 \, X_j}{\beta_j} \ge S_i \beta_i - \frac{X_0^2}{2\beta_j}$$

$$i = 1, 2, j = 1, 2 \text{ and } j \ne i \qquad (1')$$

$$(X_1 + X_0)(X_2 + X_0) \ge S_{12} \, \beta_1 \, \beta_2 + \frac{X_0^2}{2} \qquad (2')$$

$$0 \le X_i \le \beta_i \qquad\qquad i = 1, 2 \qquad (4)$$

It may be noted that the objective function of $\text{TPCT}(X_0)$ reflects the assumption regarding the form of the cost functions. Constraints (1') and (2') respectively represent service level constraints (1) and (2) for uniform distributions. The reader may find Figure 5.3.1 useful in deriving these constraints. In the figure I describe, for given values of X_0, X_1 and X_2, computation of service levels. For example, the shaded region ICDGHI includes all realizations in which the demand for both products can be satisfied. Since the demands are uniformly distributed, the joint service level achieved by investments in X_0, X_1 and X_2 is given by the area of the shaded region, normalized by scaling the axes by β_1 and β_2. Constraint (2') specifies that this should be at least as large as S_{12}, the desired level.

Similarly, demand for product 1 (product 2) may be satisfied completely (without any recourse to rationing among products) for demand realizations in the region HABCDGH (HICDEFH), and the corresponding area defines service level for product 1 (product 2). I observe that for demand realizations in the region CLDC shortages are inevitable, but that, depending on priorities, it is possible to satisfy demand for either product (but not both). Similarly, in region BJLCB(LMEDL), while it is not possible to completely satisfy the demand for product 2 (product 1), operating policies determine the extent of demand for product 1 (product 2) that may be satisfied. Clearly in the region JKMLJ, the demands are too large and shortages occur in both products. As remarked earlier, my objective in this chapter is to examine investment strategies independent of operating policies, and the service levels are defined accordingly. Thus, the actual service levels may be larger than S_1 and/or S_2, depending on the rationing policies, adopted by the management. It may be noted that constraints (1') and (2') in TPCT(X_0) are based on the implicit assumption that $X_1 + X_0 \leq \beta_i$ and $X_2 + X_0 \leq \beta_2$. When these conditions are violated, the constraints need to be modified. For the sake of brevity, I omit the details of these cases because they result in easily solvable subproblems TPCT(X_0). Instead, I focus on the analysis of the more interesting case described in Figure 5.3.1. However, I have made provision for these cases in the computational procedures and experiments described later in the chapter.

I observe that TPCT(X_0) is a non-linear program with concave objective functions and nonlinear constraints. In the remainder of this section I develop some characteristics that are useful in deriving an efficient procedure for obtaining an optimal solution to TPCT(X_0). First note that, for a given X_0, constraints (1') are linear in X_1 and X_2. Constraint (2') remain nonlinear in X_1 and X_2. However it is easy to show that the feasible region of TPCT(X_0) forms a convex set (the proof is straightforward and presented in Appendix G).

As a result, it is sufficient to restrict attention to the extreme points of the feasible set. Even though the potential number of extreme points is infinite (because of non-linear constraint (2')), the number of extreme points corresponding to intersections of tight constraints is limited (these are denoted as points P_i in the remainder of this section). In what follows, I present some results that narrow down the set of potential optimal extreme points to a maximum of five. In this development, it may be useful to refer to Figure 5.3.2, which illustrates several instances of the feasible region of TPCT(X_0).

Let $P_1 = (X_1^{(1)}, X_2^{(1)})$ be an optimal solution to TPCT(X_0) in which constraints (1') and (4) are ignored. Similarly let $P_j = (X_1^{(j)}, X_2^{(j)})$, $j = 2,..., 10$, denote extreme points obtained as intersection of constraints (1'), (2') and (4). The P_j ($j = 1, 2,..., 10$) are described in an $X_1 X_2$ plane in Figure 5.3.2. I do not consider the extreme point corresponding to $X_1 = \beta_1$, $X_2 = \beta_2$ because this solution is obviously not optimal. It may be noted that some of P_js may not be feasible and thus potential optimal solutions (feasible extreme points) are a subset of $\{P_1, P_2,..., P_{10}\}$.

Observe that it is straightforward to determine the extreme points P_1 to P_{10}. P_1 can be obtained by Lagrangian multipliers method and P_j ($j = 2,..., 10$) may be obtained directly by setting the corresponding constraints as equalities and solving for X_1 and X_2. Furthermore, simple dominant rules can be used to effectively determine the set of feasible extreme points. The details are presented below:

Solution P_1 (The optimal solution to TPCT(X_0) in which constraints (1') and (4) are ignored):

$$X_1^{(1)} = \sqrt{\frac{C_2}{C_1} (S_{12}\beta_1\beta_2 + \frac{X_0^2}{2})} - X_0$$

$$X_2^{(1)} = \sqrt{\frac{C_1}{C_2} (S_{12}\beta_1\beta_2 + \frac{X_0^2}{2})} - X_0$$

Solution P_2 (Intersection of Constraint (1') for $i = 1$ and constraint (1') for $i = 2$):

$$X_1^{(2)} = S_1\beta_1 - \frac{X_0^2}{2\beta_2} - \frac{X_0 X_2^{(2)}}{\beta_2}$$

$$X_2^{(2)} = \frac{\beta_1\beta_2 (S_2\beta_2 - S_1 X_0) + \frac{X_0^2}{2}(X_0 - \beta_2)}{\beta_1\beta_2 - X_0^2}$$

Solution P_3 (Intersection of Constraint (1') for $i = 1$ and Constraint (2')):

$$X_1^{(3)} = S_1\beta_1 - \frac{X_0^2}{2\beta_2} - \frac{X_0 X_2^{(3)}}{\beta_2}$$

$$X_2^{(3)} = \frac{S_1\beta_1\beta_2 - \frac{3}{2}X_0^2 + X_0\beta_2}{2X_0} \pm$$

$$\frac{\sqrt{(S_1\beta_1\beta_2 - \frac{3}{2}X_0^2 + X_0\beta_2)^2 - 4X_0[\beta_1\beta_2(S_{12}\beta_2 - S_1 X_0)] + \frac{X_0^2}{2}(X_0 - \beta_2)}}{2X_0}$$

Note that the above definition may result in two solutions for P_3. If only one solution is feasible, we keep the feasible one and discard the other. If both are feasible, we choose the one that results in lower costs.

Solution P_4 (Intersection of Constraint (1') for $i = 2$ and Constraint (2'))

$$X_1^{(4)} = \frac{S_2\beta_1\beta_2 - \frac{3}{2}X_0^2 + X_0\beta_1}{2X_0} \pm$$

$$\frac{\sqrt{(S_2\beta_1\beta_2 - \frac{3}{2}X_0^2 + X_0\beta_1)^2 - 4X_0[\beta_1\beta_2(S_{12}\beta_1 - S_2X_0)] + \frac{X_0^2}{2}(X_0 - \beta_1)}}{2X_0}$$

$$X_2^{(4)} = S_2\beta_2 - \frac{X_0^2}{2\beta_1} - \frac{X_0 X_1^{(4)}}{\beta_1}$$

Note that the above definition may result in two solutions for P_4. If only one solution is feasible, we keep the feasible one and discard the other. If both are feasible, we choose the one that results in lower costs.

Solution P_5 (Intersection of Constraint (1') for $i = 1$ and the upper bound in Constraints (4) for $i = 2$):

$$X_1^{(5)} = S_1\beta_1 - X_0 - \frac{X_0^2}{2\beta_2}, \quad X_2^{(5)} = \beta_2,$$

$$\text{if } S_1\beta_1 \geq X_0 + \frac{X_0^2}{2\beta_2};$$

$$X_1^{(5)} = 0, X_2^{(5)} = \frac{2S_1\beta_1\beta_2 - X_0^2}{2X_0}, \quad \text{otherwise.}$$

Notice that Solution P_5 is the intersection point of constraint (1') for $i = 1$ with constraint (4) for $i = 2$. When X_0 increases, $X_1^{(5)}$ may become negative (That is, $S_1\beta_1 - X_0 - \frac{X_0^2}{2\beta_2} < 0$). Since X_1 is restricted to be non-negative, we may obtain a non-negative solution of P_5 by obtaining an intersection point of constraint (1') and $X_1 = 0$. P_7, P_9, and P_{10} are similar to P_5.

Solution P_6 (Intersection of Constraint (1') for $i = 1$ and the lower bound in Constraints (4) for $i = 2$):

$$X_1^{(6)} = S_1\beta_1 - \frac{X_0^2}{2\beta_2}$$

$$X_2^{(6)} = 0$$

Solution P_7 (Intersection of Constraint (1') for $i = 2$ and the upper bound in Constraints (4) for $i = 1$):

$$X_1^{(7)} = \beta_1, \; X_2^{(7)} = S_2\beta_2 - X_0 - \frac{X_0^2}{2\beta_1},$$

$$\text{if } S_2\beta_2 \geq X_0 + \frac{X_0^2}{2\beta_1};$$

$$X_1^{(7)} = \frac{2S_2\beta_1\beta_2 - X_0^2}{2X_0}, \; X_2^{(7)} = 0, \qquad \text{otherwise.}$$

Solution P_8 (Intersection of Constraint (1') for $i = 2$ and the lower bound in Constraints (4) for $i = 1$):

$$X_1^{(8)} = 0$$

$$X_2^{(8)} = S_2\beta_2 - \frac{X_0^2}{2\beta_1}$$

Solution P_9 (Intersection of Constraint (2') and the upper bound of Constraints (4) for $i = 2$):

$$X_1^{(9)} = \frac{S_{12}\beta_1\beta_2 + \frac{X_0^2}{2}}{\beta_2 + X_0} - X_0,$$

$$X_2^{(9)} = \beta_2, \qquad \text{if } \frac{S_{12}\beta_1\beta_2 + \frac{X_0^2}{2}}{\beta_2 + X_0} \geq X_0;$$

$$X_1^{(9)} = 0, \; X_2^{(9)} = \frac{S_{12}\beta_1\beta_2}{X_0} - \frac{X_0}{2}, \qquad \text{otherwise.}$$

Solution P_{10} (Intersection of Constraint (2') and the upper bound of Constraint (4) for $i = 1$):

$$X_1^{(10)} = \beta_1,$$

$$X_2^{(10)} = \frac{S_{12}\beta_1\beta_2 + \dfrac{X_0^2}{2}}{\beta_1 + X_0} - X_0,$$

$$\text{if } \frac{S_{12}\beta_1\beta_2 + \dfrac{X_0^2}{2}}{\beta_1 + X_0} \geq X_0;$$

$$X_1^{(10)} = \frac{S_{12}\beta_1\beta_2}{X_0} - \frac{X_0}{2}, \quad X_2^{(10)} = 0, \qquad \text{otherwise.}$$

The following propositions demonstrate that an optimal solution to TPCT(X_0) can be found among $\{P_1, P_2,..., P_{10}\}$. They are also useful in eliminating some of these solutions and further shortening the list of candidate solutions. In this development, we make use of the fact that it is sufficient to consider investment choices in X_0 up to a level that assures all service level requirements. Clearly, this extreme strategy would require no additional investments in dedicated technologies, and further increases in X_0 are unnecessary. An upper bound on X_0, U_{X_0} may be derived easily as follows:

$$U_{X_0} = \max \{\sqrt{2\beta_1\beta_2\max\{S_{12},S_1,S_2\}},$$
$$S_1\beta_1, S_2\beta_2, \beta_1+\beta_2 - \sqrt{2\beta_1\beta_2(1-S_{12})}\}$$

The first term in the right hand side of the expression above is based on TPCT(X_0). However, as mentioned earlier, when one or both of the conditions $X_1 + S_0 \leq \beta_1$, $X_2 + X_0 \leq \beta_2$, are violated, this may not represent a valid upper bound. In such cases a valid bound may be obtained by considering the case with $X_1 = 0$ and $X_2 = 0$ and determining the amount of X_0 required to satisfy the service level constraints. The last three terms of the upper bound above follow trivially from such an analysis.

Proposition 1: Consider a relaxed version of TPCT(X_0) in which Constraints (1') and upper bounds on X_1 and X_2 (Constraints (4)) are ignored.

If $X_0 \geq \sqrt{2\beta_1\beta_2S_{12}}$, then optimal solution to TPCT (X_0) is given by $X_1 = X_2 = 0$. Otherwise, we have the following:

(i)   If fixed costs are zero, i.e., $F_i = 0$, $i = 1, 2$, P_1 is optimal for the relaxed version of TPCT(X_0).

(ii) Otherwise, optimal solution may be obtained as

$$\arg \min \{ \sum_{i=1}^{2} f_i (X_i^{(1)}), \sum_{i=1}^{2} f_i (X_i'), \sum_{i=1}^{2} f_i (X_i'') \}$$

where $X_i' = (X_1' = 0, X_2' = \dfrac{S_{12}\beta_1\beta_2}{X_0} - \dfrac{X_0}{2})$ and

$$X_i'' = (X_1'' = \dfrac{S_{12}\beta_1\beta_2}{X_0} - \dfrac{X_0}{2}, X_2'' = 0)$$

Proof: Part (i) of the proposition is a direct consequence of the following facts:

(a) Constraint (2') is tight in an optimal solution

(b) One of the two variables can be eliminated (say, X_2), and the objective value can be expressed as a function of X_1. Denote $F(X_1)$ as the objective value.

(c) $F(X_1)$ is convex in X_1 since $F''(X_1) \geq 0$.

(d) By definition of P_1, P_1 minimizes $F(X_1)$.

To see Comment (c), above note that

$$F(X_1) = C_1 X_1 + C_2 [\dfrac{A}{X_1 + X_0} - X_0] \text{ where } A = S_{12}\beta_1\beta_2 + \dfrac{X_0^2}{2}$$

(right side of Constraint (2')).

$$\text{And } F'(X_1) = C_1 - \dfrac{C_2 A}{(X_1 + X_0)^2} ; \ F''(X_1) = \dfrac{2C_2 A}{(X_1 + X_0)^3} \geq 0.$$

To prove part (ii), we note that the objective function is identical to that in part (i) except for discontinuities at X' and X''. Consequently

a direct comparison of the cost function between solution X_i', X_i'' and P_1 provides the optimal solution.

Proposition 2: Consider the problem TPCT(X_0). Suppose that either $0 < X_1^{(1)} \le X_1^{(3)}, X_1^{(4)}$; or $X_1^{(1)} \ge X_1^{(4)}, X_1^{(3)} > 0$, then

$$\sum_{i=1}^{2} f_i(X_i^{(3)}) \le \sum_{i=1}^{2} f_i (X_i^{(4)}) \text{ if } |X_1^{(3)} - X_1^{(1)}| \le |X_1^{(4)} - X_1^{(1)}|;$$

$$\sum_{i=1}^{2} f_i (X_i^{(4)}) \le \sum_{i=1}^{2} f_i (X_i^{(3)}) \text{ otherwise.}$$

Proof: The result is direct consequence of some of the results in the proof of Proposition 1. Specifically, it may be noted that

(i)   Constraint (2') is tight for solutions P_1, P_3 and P_4;
(ii) $F(X_1)$ is convex in X_1 (from the proof of Proposition 1), and
(iii) by definition, P_1 minimizes $F(X_1)$.

The proposition follows from observations of (ii) and (iii) above.

Comment: I note that the results of Proposition 1 and 2 can be modified easily without affecting the nature of the results for cases in which some X_1s or X_2s take the value of zero. This adjustment is necessary due to the fixed charge associated with the investment decisions.

Proposition 3: For TPCT(X_0), if $X_0 < UX_0$, only one of P_5, P_8 and P_9 is feasible. Similarly, only one of P_6, P_7 and P_{10} is feasible.

Proof: By definition, P_5 is the intersection of constraint (1') for $i = 1$ with $X_2 = \beta_2$; P_8 is the intersection of constraint (1') for $i = 2$ with $X_1 = 0$; P_9 is the intersection of constraint (2') with $X_2 = \beta_2$. Now consider following four mutually exclusive and totally exhaustive cases:

(i) $S_1\beta_1 \ge X_0 + \dfrac{X_0^2}{2\beta_2}$ and $\dfrac{S_{12}\beta_1\beta_2 + \dfrac{X_0^2}{2}}{\beta_2 + X_0} \ge X_0;$

(ii) $S_1\beta_1 \ge X_0 + \dfrac{X_0^2}{2\beta_2}$ and $\dfrac{S_{12}\beta_1\beta_2 + \dfrac{X_0^2}{2}}{\beta_2 + X_0} < X_0;$

(iii) $S_1\beta_1 < X_0 + \dfrac{X_0^2}{2\beta_2}$ and $\dfrac{S_{12}\beta_1\beta_2 + \dfrac{X_0^2}{2}}{\beta_1 + X_0} \geq X_0;$

(iv) $S_1\beta_1 < X_0 + \dfrac{X_0^2}{2\beta_2}$ and $\dfrac{S_{12}\beta_1\beta_2 + \dfrac{X_0^2}{2}}{\beta_1 + X_0} < X_0.$

In the first case, $X_2^{(5)} = X_2^{(9)} = \beta_2$.

Thus P_8 is infeasible since $X_1^{(8)} = 0$ and $X_2^{(8)} \leq \beta_2$ do not satisfy constraints (1') and (2'). If $X_1^{(5)} = X_1^{(9)}$, P_5 and P_9 are identical. If $X_1^{(5)} > X_1^{(9)}$, obviously P_9 can not satisfy constraints (1') and (2'). Thus P_9 is infeasible and P_5 is the only feasible solution. Otherwise, P_9 is the only feasible solution. Similarly, we can show that only one solution of P_5, P_8 and P_9 is feasible in cases (ii), (iii) and (iv). The same argument can apply to P_6, P_7 and P_{10}.

The properties above together imply that at most five of the ten extreme points (P_1, P_2, ..., P_{10}) are feasible. Further, the propositions permit elimination of some of these extreme points as candidates for optimal solution. I develop an effective search method to find the optimal solution for a TPCT(X_0). Figure 5.3.3 describes a general scheme that simplifies the search process. The search procedure starts finding dominant relationships among three extreme points of P_2, P_5 and P_7 (see Appendix H for an illustrative example).

5.4 A SOLUTION PROCEDURE FOR TPCT

In this section I present a solution procedure that is based on the analysis of TPCT(X_0) discussed in Section 3. The procedure involves linear search over X_0, the amount of flexible technology used, and is based on the following equivalent formulation of TPCT:

(TPCT) $Z_{TPCT} = $ Min: $f_0(X_0) + F(X_0)$

Subject to: $0 \leq X_0 \leq U_{X_0}$

where U_{X_0} is the upper bound of X_0, discussed in the previous section.

I note that since we permit concave cost functions, in general, the objective function of TPCT, $f_0(X_0) + F(X_0)$, is not convex in X_0 and it is necessary to search over the full range of X_0. I propose to obtain a value of X_0 that is within a parameter Δ of the optimal value by searching over X_0 in increments of Δ. The solution procedure may be summarized as follows:

Step 0: Set Δ and U_{X_0}; $X_0 = 0$; obtain $F(X_0)$ for $X_0 = 0$ and X_1 and X_2 when $X_0 = 0$. $F(X_0 = 0)$ is current optimal objective value for TPCT.

Step 1: Let $X_0 = X_0 + \Delta$ and solve TPCT(X_0) optimally using procedure described in Figure 5.3.3.

Step 2: If $f_0(X_0) + F(X_0)$ improves current optimal objective value, update the objective value and solutions and go to step 3. Otherwise, go to step 3.

Step 3: If $X_0 + \Delta \leq U_{X_0}$, go to step 1. Otherwise, stop.

It should be noted that if necessary, the procedure above may be repeated to find a more accurate optimal X_0. For example, if an approximate optimal X_0 has been located, we may improve the accuracy by redefining lower and upper bounds of X_0 that are close to the current approximate optimal X_0 and successively reducing the increment size. For the implementation of this procedure (for experiments·described in the next section), I have incorporated other refinements to reduce the computational burden. For example, in some cases, for specific values of X_0 it is possible to identify redundant constraints that simplify the resulting subproblems. These modifications do not provide much insights and we omit the details for the sake of brevity.

I conclude this section by noting that my choice of a linear search procedure for X_0 was motivated by convenience. If necessary, this procedure could be replaced by one of the efficient procedures available in the literature. In our experiments, computational time was not a major issue and hence it was not necessary to explore alternative methods. In addition to providing the optimal value of X_0, our procedure derives total cost as a function of X_0. This may provide additional information in understanding the tradeoffs associated with flexible capacity.

5.5   COMPUTATIONAL   RESULTS

In this section, I present results of computational experiments designed to illustrate the application of the procedures developed in this paper for examining the tradeoffs between the costs and the benefits of flexible technology. The results also provide some insights on the role of flexible technology under a variety of conditions.

In the design of the test problems I focused on cost functions and demand parameters β_1 and β_2. The desired service levels were set at S_1 = 0.9, S_2 = 0.85 and S_{12} = 0.80. In this experiment, I considered three types of cost functions--linear, fixed charge and power cost (Cobb-Douglas) functions, and I generated a total of 320 test problems. In the problems with linear costs, the unit costs of dedicated technologies (c_1 and c_2) were set at 100 while the unit cost of flexible technology (c_0) was varied between 100 and 200 in steps of 20, thus providing six cost functions. It may be noted that this choice of parameters provides a wide range of costs, with c_0 = 100 (200) representing the extreme case in which all (zero) flexible technology is optimal. These extreme cases were used as benchmarks in evaluating the optimal choices for the other cases. In addition, I also examined two sets of fixed-charge cost functions. Two levels of fixed charge were considered in order to study the impact of the fixed-cost on the role of flexible technology. My choice of parameters was based on the examples presented in Luss (1980).

In the choice of the power cost function, I considered two levels of economies of scale, and the parameter α was set at 0.9 and 0.95. The cost of flexible technology relative to dedicated capacity ranged between 1.2 and 1.4. As detailed in Table 1, I chose a total of eight cost functions.

In order to design test problems with a wide range of values for demand parameters β_1 and β_2, I used two methods to generate a total of 20 pairs of values for β_1 and β_2. In the first method (referred to as independent parameters) ten pairs of values were chosen from a discrete uniform distribution between 1 and 50. In the second method (referred to as dependent parameters) I generated 10 pairs of values in the following manner:

(i) A number representing ($\beta_1 + \beta_2$) was randomly generated from a discrete uniform distribution between 1 and 100.
(ii) The proportion of demand for product 1, P_1, was chosen randomly between 0 and 1.0. β_1 was then determined as $P_1 * (\beta_1 + \beta_2)$ and β_2 = $(1 - P_1) * (\beta_1 + \beta_2)$. In these problems, the choice of β_1 and β_2 was

restricted to integer values, by rounding off, where necessary. (The reader may note that, while β_1 and β_2 are dependent in the second set, the demand distributions are assumed to be independent with parameters β_1 and β_2.)

The set of 20 values of β_1 and β_2, together with the 16 cost functions described earlier, gives rise to 320 test problems for this experiment. Table 5.5.1 presents the details of the data used in the test problems. In addition to obtaining the optimal solution for each problem, I also computed the cost of all flexible technology and zero flexible technology strategy. For the sake of brevity, I do not provide the details of the solutions. Instead, I provide summary results in Tables 5.5.2 and 5.5.3 and discuss briefly some interesting conclusions. These are based on the following four performance measures:

(a) The amount of flexible capacity as a % of total capacity (Flex Cap).
(b) The cost of investment in flexible capacity as a % of total investment (Flex Cost).
(c) The % increase in cost of all flexible technology strategy, relative to the optimal plan (All Flex).
(d) The % increase in cost of an inflexible technology strategy, relative to the optimal plan (All Ded).

For the ten problems defined by each cost function and (β_1, β_2) pairs (either dependent or independent), the average of the above four measures are presented in Tables 5.5.2 and 5.5.3. The results suggest some interesting conclusions that are briefly discussed below.

(1) Investments in flexible technology are economically justified even in the absence of scale economies. For example, except for the extreme case when $c_0 = 200$, even with linear costs the measures Flex Cap and Flex Cost are positive with up to 20% of additions in flexible capacity. This is indicative of the importance of product-mix flexibility in meeting uncertain demands.

(2) The amount of flexible capacity (Flex Cap) increases with scale economies. This result, which is fairly intuitive, is observed with both fixed-charge and power-cost functions. However, even small increases in scale economies result in disproportionately large increases in the use of flexible capacity. For example, a decrease in α from 0.95 to 0.9 results in an increase of Flex Cap from 60% to 77%. Such large increases are counter-intuitive and provide a case for the need for model-based support for making these strategic decisions.

(3) The method for generating demand parameters β_1 and β_2 does not appear to have any significant impact on the four performance measures. This is not very surprising, since product demands are assumed to be independent. It is encouraging to note that relative differences between β_1 and β_2 (in the test problems considered in this experiment) do not have appreciable effect. However, I conjecture that dependency between product demands is an important factor and will have a significant impact on the role of flexible capacity.

(4) The results indicate that even in an environment with independent, static demands, there is a need for an appropriate mix of dedicated and flexible technology. Measures All Flex and All Ded indicate that a strategy which ignores these considerations could result in significant cost penalties. My results also suggest that, except when flexible technology is inexpensive, relatively small amounts of flexible capacity is usually sufficient. In such cases, dedicated technologies are used to satisfy most of the product demand. Flexible capacity plays the role of "cushion" and is just enough to account for the uncertainties in product demands. Other factors such as scale economies (considered in my model) and demand dependencies (not considered in my model) affect these results and may result in higher levels of investment in flexible capacity. Some of these conclusions are borne out by my computational results.

I conclude this section by noting that the computational results of this section support the need for a systematic approach for understanding the economies and the tradeoffs involved in technology and capacity decisions. As elaborated earlier, these choices depend on a number of factors. While the qualitative influence of these factors is fairly well understood, my results suggest that more specifics are needed for making these decisions. The approach and the procedures presented in this chapter are useful in this context for developing, in specific instances, a better understanding of the issues involved in these strategic choices.

5.6   CONCLUSIONS

Empirical studies in recent years examining practices influencing technology choice and capacity decisions have identified, among others, two factors responsible for the slow adoption of modern flexible technologies by American firms (in comparison with the Japanese and Europeans). While one of these factors (scale economies) is usually explicitly considered in evaluation methods, the other (scope economies) is not. In contrast, academic literature dealing with flexible technologies usually assumes linear or convex costs. In this chapter, I develop an investment model that incorporates these two factors, and provide a method to determine the optimal mix of technology and capacity choices in an environment characterized by two-product families with stochastic demands. While the inclusion of scale economies results in a model that is intractable for deriving analytical results, my detailed analysis of a special case suggests that my approach could be used to develop a managerial tool for understanding the related tradeoffs in specific cases.

While the two-product problem described in this chapter is interesting in its own right and has potential for applications, my objective is to use the model and the results as a building block in the development of a general model that can be used as a framework for examining issues related to technology and capacity choices. Thus, it would be worthwhile to explore extensions of the model in several directions. While some of these are straightforward, others are more complex and require significant research effort. For example, it is possible to include the following features without increasing the complexity of the model:

(i)   operating costs that depend on production levels
(ii) salvage costs of equipment at the end of planning horizon
(iii) depreciation of equipment resulting in loss of capacity

More challenging tasks relate to extensions of the model to more than two products, to other demand distributions, and to dynamic demands. Because of its popularity, analysis with normal distribution would be of particular interest. Another important feature relates to provision for dependence in product demands. While the model TPCT presented in Section 2 does not preclude such dependencies, development of solution procedures is strongly influenced by demand distributions and the nature of dependencies. Thus, I expect extensions in the context to be application specific. Clearly, such extensions are non-trivial and require additional research effort. Finally, it may be noted that in some of these cases it may be necessary to include explicitly allocation decisions resulting in more complex problems.

VI. CONCLUSION

6.1 SUMMARY

This chapter concludes the present study of heuristic approaches for deriving investment plans and making technology choices and describing the tradeoffs between cost and manufacturing flexibility. I developed several investment models that make a contribution to the evaluation of flexible technologies in discrete manufacturing systems. I have demonstrated that manufacturing flexibility is economically justified under both deterministic and stochastic environments. The approximation approaches are easy-to-implement tools that can support management investment decisions in production capacity over medium- and long-term planning horizons. In comparison with exact (analytical) results and lower bounds, my computational results show that these approaches work very well. I have also conducted extensive computational experiments to derive manufacturing capacity strategies.

6.2 FUTURE RESEARCH

There exist several avenues for future research. These avenues fall into three major categories: modelling and algorithm development, empirical studies, and applications.

Flexible technologies are particularly useful in stochastic environments that are characterized by uncertainty. An important extension of the current research is the development of capacity expansion and technology selection models with multiple products or other uncertainties. As shown in Chapter 5, a stochastic investment model with only two products is very difficult to solve. Model with multiple products may involve more issues in the determination of optimal solutions. Thus both analytical results and solution procedures are to be developed. Incorporation of uncertainty in acquisition costs as well as complexity of new technologies into my current model will be very important in the context of technology management. Further my current model can be modified to relate to integration of technology and expansion choices with marketing decisions. In such scenarios, the objective is to choose demand and price levels and appropriate mix of production technologies. Hence, extensions which incorporate these factors will result in a comprehensive model that permits simultaneous evaluation of several key elements.

Although the case of uncertain demands has been examined by several researchers, stochastic and dynamic demand patterns in the case of multiple products and multiple periods has been studied by few researchers. A valuable extension then would be an investment model with stochastic and dynamic demands. The investment model that has been developed in the present study considers stochastic and dynamic demand patterns. However, this model requires pre-allocation of capacities. Development of a model with relaxation of that restriction and with solution procedures will make a very important contribution to the research in this area.

I have conducted extensive computational experiments to test my heuristics. The computational results from these experiments may help us to study the investment behavior or explore strategies in investment decisions. Two extreme scenarios may be examined: deterministic and stochastic environments. In both environments, a number of factors influence strategic choices related to technology selection and capacity additions. These include, among others, product mix characteristics, technology alternatives, cost parameters, demand patterns, and length of the planning horizon, etc. Thus, development of capacity expansion and technology selection strategies considering all these factors will be very helpful to practitioner to understand implication of our mathematical models and will also provide a meaningful linkage between quantitative approaches and conceptual work.

Possible application of our models and heuristics developed should be explored. In these situations, the solutions themselves are of paramount interest in contrast with the computational experiments described in the previous chapters where the solutions were not *useful* in practice.

Table 3.5: Summary of Computational Results

Cost Set	Case	Demand Pattern	No.	No. of Prob. with Optimal Solution			Avg. Relative Error of Heuristics			Max. Relative Error		Avg. Deviation from LB	
				Toal	SMCP	SP	Better of Two	SMCP	SP	SMCP	SP	SMCP	SP
I	(a)	Independent	10	5	2	5	0.326%	1.544%	0.333%	3.694%	2.369%	8.502%	7.716%
	(b)	Dependent I	10	5	0	5	0.365%	2.373%	0.460%	4.528%	1.849%	9.610%	7.496%
	(c)	Dependent II	10	5	1	4	0.406%	1.586%	0.491%	3.026%	2.232%	9.510%	8.370%
II	(a)	Independent	10	5	5	3	0.999%	2.268%	1.841%	7.89%	4.38%	18.92%	19.12%
	(b)	Dependent I	10	8	4	5	0.215%	2.099%	1.366%	5.27%	6.22%	21.10%	19.66%
	(c)	Dependent II	10	0	0	5	1.615%	7.23%	1.615%	13.80%	7.07%	21.88%	15.49%
Total Number			60	33	12	27							

Note:
i. Cost set I corresponds to cost functions 40+8x and 30+7x for dedicated and flexible technologies.
   Cost set II corresponds to cost functions 4000+24x and 3700+18x for dedicated and flexible technologies.
ii. Dependent I and II correspond to μ_{p1} equal to 0.5 and 0.7.
iii. Better of Two under Avg. Relative Error of Heuristics is calculated by choosing the better of the two final solutions obtained through SMCP and SP respectively.
iv. LB refers to Lower Bound.

Table 4.4.1: Design of Computational Experiments

Experiment	I	II	III
Planning Horizon	5	5	10
No. of Product	3	3	5
Cost Function K_0	1.05, 1.2	1.05, 1.2	1.2
α	0.8, 0.9	0.8, 0.9, 0.95	0.8, 0.9
Demand Independ.	$d_{ik} = 1.0t\xi_{xt}$	$d_{ik} = 5.0t\xi_{xt}$	$d_{ik} = 3.0t\xi_{xt}$
Pattern Depend.	$D_t = 3.0t\xi_{xt}$ $d_{ik} = P_{ik}D_t$	$D_t = 15.0t\xi_{xt}$ $d_{ik} = P_{ik}D_t$	$D_t = 15.0t\xi_{xt}$ $d_{ik} = P_{ik}D_t$
Optimal Solution	Available	Not Available	Not Available

1. $K_i = 1.0$ for $i = 1, 2.$

Computational Experiments with Fixed Charge Cost Function

Experiment	IV	V	VI
Planning Horizon	5	5	10
Cost Functions	a $f_i(\cdot) = 30 + 7X$ $f_0(\cdot) = 40 + 8X$ b $f_i(\cdot) = 30 + 8X$ $f_0(\cdot) = 45 + 9.6X$ c $f_i(\cdot) = 1 + 5X$ $f_0(\cdot) = 1.5 + 5.5X$ d $f_i(\cdot) = 1 + 7X$ $f_0(\cdot) = 1.3 + 8X$	a $f_i(\cdot) = 30 + 7X$ $f_0(\cdot) = 40 + 8X$ b $f_i(\cdot) = 30 + 8X$ $f_0(\cdot) = 45 + 9.6X$	a $f_i(\cdot) = 30 + 7X$ $f_0(\cdot) = 40 + 8X$ b $f_i(\cdot) = 30 + 8X$ $f_0(\cdot) = 45 + 9.6X$
Demand Independ.	$d_{ik} = 1.0t\xi_{xt}$	$d_{ik} = 5.0t\xi_{xt}$	$d_{ik} = 3.0t\xi_{xt}$
Pattern Depend.	$D_t = 3.0t\xi_{xt}$ $d_{ik} = P_{ik}D_t$	$D_t = 15.0t\xi_{xt}$ $d_{ik} = P_{ik}D_t$	$D_t = 15.0t\xi_{xt}$ $d_{ik} = P_{ik}D_t$
Optimal Solution	Available	Available	Not Available

2. $f_i(\cdot)$ is the cost function for dedicated technology, $\forall$ i; $f_0(\cdot)$ is that for flexible technology.

Note:

The basic demand pattern is $bt\xi_t$ where b is a growth parameter, t is a time period and ξ_t is a normally distributed random variable with mean of 1.0 and a standard deviation of 0.1 (the range of variation of ξ_t is between 0.7 and 1.3.)

(a) Independent demand: The demand for each product family grows following the equation of $bt\xi_t$.

(b) Dependent demand: The total demand of all product i families (denoted as D_t) follows $D_t\xi_t$. P_{it} is the proportion of demand due to product i in period t (That is, $d_{it} = P_{it}D_t$). P_{it} is generated in the following manner: (i) a random variable P'_{it} with mean of 1/N and a standard deviation of 0.1 is generated; (ii) P_{it} is equal to $(1/\sum_{i=1}^{N} P'_{it})P_{it}$. The dependent demand pattern, as a result, is more erratic than the independent pattern.

Table 4.4.1a: Summary Results of Experiment with Power Cost Functions (3 products, 5 periods)

α for All Technologies	Demand Pattern	Avg. Relative Error of Heuristic	Max Relative Error	Avg. Dev. of Optimals to Dual LB	Avg. Dev. of Heuristics to Dual LB	Avg. Dev. of Heuristics to Agg. LB	No. of Prob. with Optimal Solutions
0.8	Independent	0.00%	0.00%	10.74%	10.74%	18.32%	10
	Dependent	0.11%	1.09%	11.44%	11.57%	17.56%	9
0.9	Independent	0.07%	0.44%	4.98%	5.05%	8.81%	8
	Dependent	0.17%	0.63%	5.07%	5.25%	8.63%	5

Note:
1. For each α , 10 problems were tested. for each demand pattern.
2. K for flexible technology in all test problems is 1.2.
3. LB means lower bound and Avg. Dev. means average deviation
4. Dual LB means lower bounds obtained by the Dual Lower Bound.
5. Agg. LB means lower bounds obtained by the Aggregate Lower Bound.

Table 4.4.1b: Summary Results of Experiment with Fixed Charge Cost Functions (3 products, 5 periods)

Prob. Set	Cost Set	Demand Pattern	Avg. Relative . Error of Heuristics (%)	Max. Relative Error of Heuristics (%)	Avg. Dev. of Heuristics to Dual LB	Avg. Dev. of Heuristics to Agg. LB	No. of Prob. with Optimal Solutions
I	I	Independent	0.00	0.00	1.76	4.20	10
		Dependent	0.00	0.00	1.93	4.61	10
	II	Independent	0.00	0.00	3.03	4.34	10
		Dependent	0.00	0.00	3.46	4.43	.10
	III	Independent	0.63	1.83	0.00	26.53	4
		Dependent	0.26	0.89	0.00	25.87	5
	IV	Independent	0.15	0.52	0.00	18.88	6
		Dependent	0.39	1.08	0.00	18.43	4
II	I	Independent	0.09	0.29	8.78	10.09	6
		Dependent	0.00	0.00	9.45	10.64	10
	II	Independent	0.01	0.29	11.22	12.46	6
		Dependent	0.02	0.24	9.06	13.13	9
			0.13				90

Note:
1. Prob. Set I refers to the 3 product, 5 period test problems with small size.
   Prob. Set II refers to the 3 product, 5 period test problems with larger size.
2. Cost Set I refers to 40+8X and 30+7X; Cost Set II refers to 45+9.6X and 30+8X; Cost Set III refers to 1.3+8X and 1.0+7X; Cost Set IV refers to 1.5+5.5X and 1.0+5.0X.
3. LB means lower bound and Avg. Dev. means average deviation.
4. Dual LB means lower bounds obtained by the Dual Lower Bound.
5. Agg. LB means lower bounds obtained by the Aggregate Lower Bound.

Table 4.4.1c: Summary Results of Experiment with Power Cost
Functions (3 products, 5 periods)

K for Flexible Technology	α for All Technologies	Demand Pattern	Avg. % of Flexible Capacity to the Total Capacity	Avg. Dev. of Heuristics to Agg. LB
1.05	0.8	Independent Dependent	100.00 100.00	5.00% 5.00%
	0.9	Independent Dependent	42.39 65.11	3.49% 4.06%
	0.95	Independent Dependent	24.00 29.00	2.27% 2.72%
1.20	0.8	Independent Dependent	65.41 65.77	19.01% 18.56%
	0.9	Independent Dependent	22.77 24.11	9.08% 9.96%
	0.95	Independent Dependent	7.25 19.41	5.16% 7.09%

Note:
1. For each K and each α , 10 problems were tested for each demand pattern.

Table 4.4.1d: Summary Results of Experiment with Power Cost
Functions (5 products, 10 periods)

K for Flexible Technology	α for All Technologies	Demand Pattern	Avg. % of Flexible Capacity to the Total Capacity	Avg. Dev. of Heuristics to Agg. LB
1.2	0.8	Independent Dependent	51.12 59.25	17.39% 17.58%
	0.9	Independent Dependent	15.72 19.22	10.11% 11.45%

Note:
1. For each α , 10 problems were tested for each demand pattern.

Table 4.4.1e: Summary Results of Experiment with Fixed Charge
Cost Functions (5 products, 10 periods)

Cost Set	Demand Pattern	Avg. % of Flexible Capacity to the Total Capacity	Avg. Dev. of Heuristics to Agg. LB. (%)
I	Independent Dependent	31.79 43.10	10.74 11.61
II	Independent Dependent	21.52 28.80	12.28 13.91

Note:
1. For each cost set, 10 problems were tested for each demand pattern.
2. Cost Set I refers to 40+8X and 30+7X; Cost Set II refers to 45+9.6X and 30+8X.

Table 5.5.1: Data for the Computational Study

Service Level: $S_1 = 0.90, S_2 = 0.85, S_{12} = 0.8$
Demand Parameters: (β_1, β_2)

Case		1	2	3	4	5	6	7	8	9	10
Independent Parameters	β_1	30	35	41	40	28	14	33	17	9	34
	β_2	30	28	9	7	31	2	32	5	19	31
Dependent Parameters	β_1	14	18	46	63	21	63	29	5	10	25
	β_2	12	51	20	12	62	11	18	2	23	5

Cost Functions:

	Linear Costs						Fixed Charge	
	F1	F2	F3	F4	F5	F6	F7	F8
Flexible	100	120	140	160	180	200	4 + 10x	40 + 8x
Dedicated	100	100	100	100	100	100	3 + 7x	30 + 7x
	Power Cost Function*							
	F1	F2	F3	F4	F5	F6	F7	F8
Parameter α	0.9	0.9	0.9	0.9	0.95	0.95	0.95	0.95
K_F	1.2	1.3	1.35	1.4	1.20	1.30	1.35	1.40

* The cost functions for dedicated and flexible technologies are respectively given by $K_D x^\alpha$ and $K_F x^\alpha$. $K_D = 1$ in all the examples.

Table 5.5.2:   Computational Results for Linear and Fixed Charge Cost
               Functions

Demand Pattern	Performance Measure	Cost Function							
		F1	F2	F3	F4	F5	F6	F7	F8
Independent	Flex Cap	100	19.33	17.01	8.00	5.69	0.00	13.27	100
	Flex Cost	100	22.72	22.07	11.89	9.64	0.00	18.04	100
	All Flex	0	3.66	16.74	30.80	45.18	60.63	15.94	0.0
	All Ded	24.85	7.70	3.91	1.82	0.40	0.0	2.20	15.52
Dependent	Flex Cap	100	19.18	14.46	7.18	3.82	0.00	10.96	100
	Flex Cost	100	22.09	19.02	11.00	6.61	0.00	15.22	100
	All Flex	0	4.34	18.13	32.31	47.24	63.0	16.93	0.0
	All Ded	22.76	6.64	3.45	1.36	0.26	0.0	1.60	22.76

Table 5.5.3:   Computational Results for Power Cost Functions

Demand Pattern	Performance Measure	Cost Function							
		F1	F2	F3	F4	F5	F6	F7	F8
Independent	Flex Cap	82.51	54.731	41.296	12.278	66.304	18.33	17.29	4.705
	Flex Cost	83.893	56.857	42.851	17.274	67.737	3.695	22.21	7.108
	All Flex	0.664	2.315	5.01	8.293	2.282	6.055	9.47	12.376
	All Ded	8.431	2.623	0.573	0.222	7.521	3.50	2.602	1.848
Dependent	Flex Cap	75.89	38.733	23.77	10.22	58.107	16.229	14.84	2.565
	Flex Cost	76.905	42.019	17.114	14.622	59.957	20.943	19.883	4.033
	All Flex	0.416	3.467	6.478	13.829	1.699	7.181	10.458	10.113
	All Ded	6.491	1.676	0.329	1.610	6.070	3.055	2.291	0.05

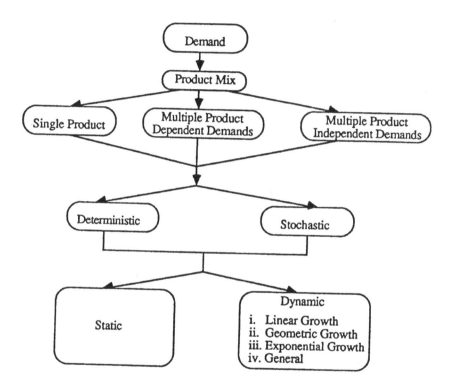

Figure 2.1a: Multi-Dimensioned Attributes of Demand

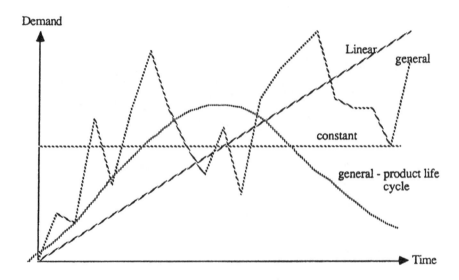

Figure 2.1b: Some Sample Demand Patterns

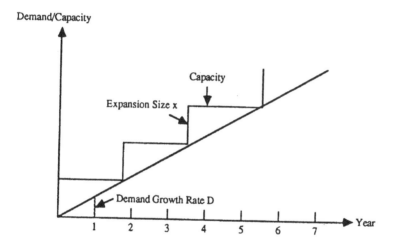

Figure 2.2.2: Process of Demand Growth and
Capacity Expansion

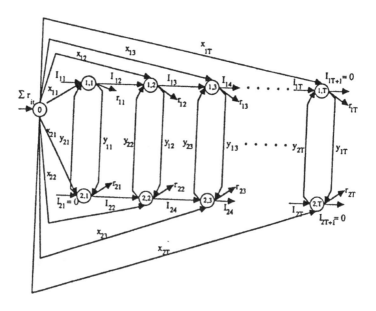

Figure 2.2.3.1: A Network-Flow Representation for
Problem LS

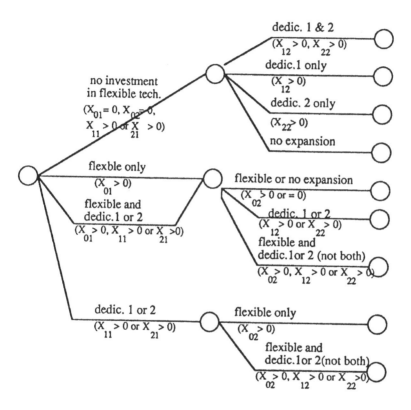

Figure 3.3.1: The Alternative Expansion Strategies

Note:
(i) The variables not presented in the above tree are assumed
to take values of zero.
(ii) In the nine strategies, $X_{it} > 0$ (i = 0, 1, 2 and t = 1, 2)
means that the strategy requires a positive investment in i
at period t assuming that there is a positive demand d_{it}. If
there is no positive d_{it}, the corresponding strategy can be
skipped.

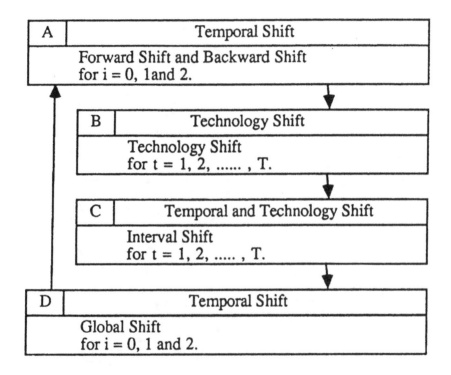

Figure 3.4.1: Improvement Heuristic Procedures

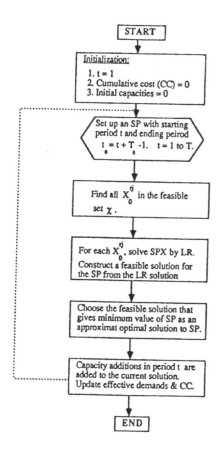

Figure 4.2.1: Initial Solution for CP (Phase I)

Note:
(i) LR refers to Lagrangian Relaxation
(ii) U_{0r} is the upper bound of X_{0r}. $U_{0r} = \max\{0,$

$$\max_{1 \leq q \leq t_e} \{\sum_{i=1}^{N} d'_{iq}\} - C_{0t-1}\}$$ where d'_{iq} is the effective demand

for product family i in period q based on capacity additions in technology i up to period (t-1), and C_{0t-1} is the cumulative flexible capacity.

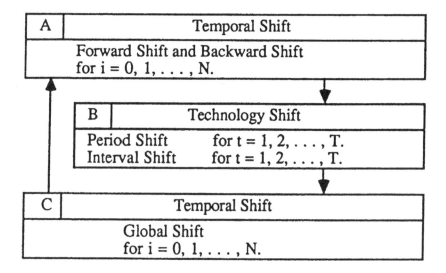

Figure 4.2.2: Improvement Heuristic Procedures (Phase II)

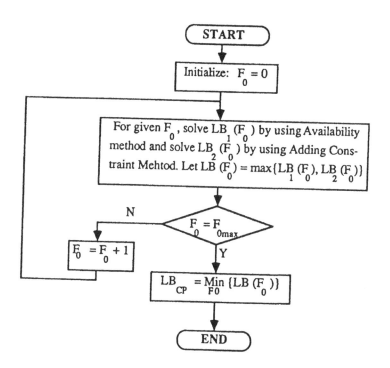

Figure 4.3.2: The Lower Bound of CP

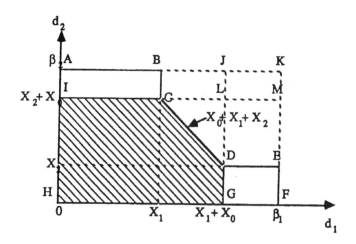

Figure 5.3.1: Feasible Region for Model TPCT

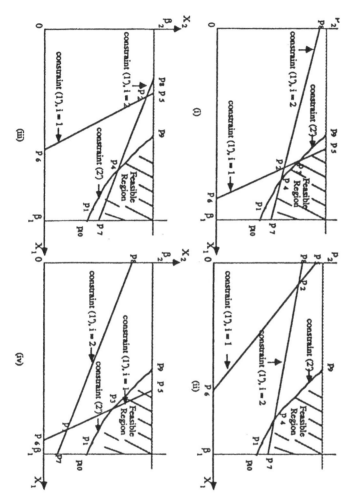

Figure 5.3.2: Feasible Regions for T(X₀)

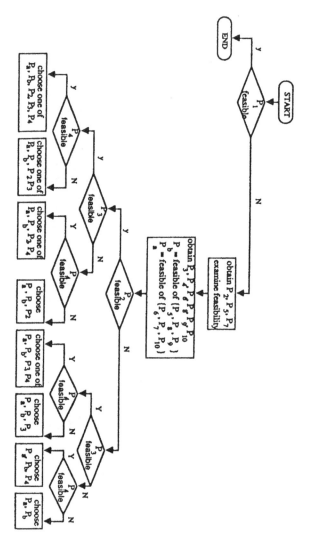

Figure 5.3.3: Flow Chart of the Search Procedure for T(X₀)

APPENDIXES

Appendix A

Proof of Proposition 1 in Chapter 3:

Proof:
1. Let X'_{it} ($i = 0, 1, 2$; $t = 1, 2,..., T$), Y'_{it} ($i = 1, 2$; $t = 1, 2,..., T$) denote a feasible solution to **CP**. We define a corresponding solution X''_{it} ($i = 0, 1, 2$; $t = 1, 2, ..., T$) for **MCP** in the following manner:

$$X''_{it} = X'_{it} \qquad \forall \; i, t.$$

Clearly, if (X', Y') is feasible for **CP**, the corresponding solution X'' is feasible for **MCP**. Further, the objective function value is the same for both solutions.

2. Let X''_{it} ($i = 0, 1, 2$; $t = 1, 2,..., T$) denote a feasible solution for **MCP**. Define a corresponding solution X'_{it} ($i = 0, 1, 2$; $t = 1, 2,...,$ T), Y'_{it} ($i = 1, 2$; $t = 1, 2,..., T$) for **CP** in the following manner:

$$X'_{it} = X''_{it} \qquad \forall \; i, t. \qquad\qquad (a.1)$$

$$Y'_{it} = \max \; \{0, d_{it} - \sum_{\tau=1}^{t} X'_{i\tau}\} \qquad i = 1, 2; \; t = 1, 2,..., \; T$$

$$(a.2)$$

Since X'' is feasible for **MCP**, X''_{it} satisfy constraints (5), (6) and (7) in **MCP**.

By definition of Y'_{it}, we have the following:

(i) $Y'_{it} \geq d_{it} - \sum_{\tau=1}^{t} X'_{i\tau}$ which implies that constraint (1) in **CP** is satisfied.

(ii) $Y'_{it} \geq 0$ which indicates that constraint (4) in **CP** is satisfied.

123

(iii) If $Y'_{it} > 0$, then $\sum\limits_{\tau=1}^{t} X'_{i\tau} + Y'_{it} = d_{it}$

(iv) If $\sum\limits_{\tau=1}^{t} X'_{i\tau} \geq d_{it}$, then $Y'_{it} = 0$

(v) Observations (iii), (iv) and constraint (5) in **MCP** imply that

$$Y'_{it} \leq \sum_{\tau=0}^{t} X'_{0\tau}.$$

Clearly, the observations above show that X', Y' satisfy constraints (1), (3) and (4) in **CP**. To see that Y' satisfy (2) in **CP**, consider the following cases:

(a) $Y'_{1t}, Y'_{2t} = 0$:
   The constraint (3) in **CP** is satisfied trivially.

(b) $Y'_{1t} > 0, Y'_{2t} = 0$: $\sum\limits_{i=1}^{2} Y'_{it} = Y'_{1t} \leq \sum\limits_{\tau=0}^{t} X'_{0\tau}$
   (by observation v)

(c) $Y'_{1t} = 0, Y'_{2t} > 0$: $\sum\limits_{i=1}^{2} Y_{it} = Y'_{2t} \leq \sum\limits_{\tau=0}^{t} X'_{0\tau}$
   (by observation v)

(d) $Y'_{1t} > 0, Y'_{2t} > 0$: $\sum\limits_{i=1}^{2}\sum\limits_{\tau=1}^{t} X'_{i\tau} + \sum\limits_{i=1}^{2} Y'_{it} = \sum\limits_{i=1}^{2} d_{it}$

$$\leq \sum_{i=1}^{2}\sum_{\tau=1}^{t} X'_{i\tau} + \sum_{\tau=0}^{t} X'_{0\tau}$$

(The equality follows from observation (iii), and the inequality follows from constrains (6) in **MCP**.) This implies that \i\su(i=1,2,)

$$Y'_{it} \leq \sum_{\tau=0}^{t} X'_{0\tau}.$$

Again note that X" and the corresponding solution X' and Y' have the same objective value. Therefore, (1) and (2) together imply that **CP** and **MCP** are equivalent.

Appendix B

Consider the following example:

$d_{11} = 1$, $d_{21} = 3$, $d_{12} = 5$, $d_{22} = 7$ and $X_{00} = 2$.

If the expansion strategy is no investment in flexible technology, then $X_{01} = 0$, $X_{02} = 0$ and $X_{11} > 0$ or $X_{21} > 0$ in the first period. If alternative one is followed, then $X_{12} > 0$ and $X_{22} > 0$.

Thus, the resulting constraints for the SMCP is as follows:

$$X_{11} \geq \max\{d_{11} - X_{00}, 0\} = 0$$

$$X_{21} \geq \max\{d_{21} - X_{00}, 0\} = 1 \quad \text{period one}$$

$$X_{11} + X_{21} = d_{11} + d_{21} - X_{00} = 2$$

$$X_{11} + X_{12} \geq \max\{d_{12} - X_{00}, 0\} = 3$$

$$X_{21} + X_{22} \geq \max\{d_{22} - X_{00}, 0\} = 5 \quad \text{Period}$$

$$X_{11} + X_{12} + X_{21} + X_{22} \geq d_{12} + d_{22} - X_{00} = 10$$
two

Obviously, the above two-period problem can be solved sequentially with two extreme points in the first period and two extreme points in the second period. The total four extreme points are as follows:

(1)	(2)	(3)	(4)
$X_{11} = 0$	$X_{11} = 0$	$X_{11} = 1$	$X_{11} = 1$
$X_{21} = 2$	$X_{21} = 2$	$X_{21} = 1$	$X_{21} = 1$
$X_{12} = 3$	$X_{12} = 5$	$X_{12} = 4$	$X_{12} = 2$
$X_{22} = 5$	$X_{22} = 3$	$X_{22} = 4$	$X_{22} = 6$

Appendix C

Consider the following example:

$d_{11} = 7, d_{12} = 4, d_{13} = 10, d_{14} = 8; d_{21} = 3, d_{22} = 6, d_{23} = 9,$
$d_{24} = 15;$

$T_s = 4, t_0 = 2, t_1 = 1, t_2 = 3$ and $X_{00} = 3.$

The resulting SP(2,1,3) may be formulated as follows:

Min: $f_{02} (X_{02}) + f_{11} (X_{11}) + f_{23} (X_{23})$

s.t. $X_{11} \geq \max\{d_{11} - X_{00}, d_{11} + d_{21} - X_{00}, 0\} = 7$ (1)

$X_{02} \geq \max\{d_{22} - X_{00}, 0\} = 3$ (2)

$X_{11} + X_{02} \geq \max\{d_{12} - X_{00}, d_{13} - X_{00}, d_{14} - X_{00},$

$d_{12} + d_{22} - X_{00}, 0\} = 7$ (3)

$X_{23} + X_{02} \geq \max\{d_{23} - X_{00}, d_{24} - X_{00}, 0\} = 12$ (4)

$X_{11} + X_{23} + X_{02} \geq \max\{d_{13} + d_{23} - X_{00}, d_{14} + d_{24} - X_{00}, 0\} = 20$

(5)

$X_{02}, X_{11}, X_{23} \geq 0$ (6)

If (1) is set at strict equality, (3) and (4) become redundant and (2), (5), (6) are modified as follows:

$X_{02} \geq 3$

$X_{23} + X_{02} \geq 13$

$X_{02}, X_{23} \geq 0$

The corresponding extreme points are:

(1) $X_{02} = 13$, $X_{11} = 7$, $X_{23} = 0$; (2) $X_{02} = 3$, $X_{11} = 7$, $X_{23} = 10$.

Similarly, if each of (2), (3), (4), and (5) is binding, the resulting extreme points are as follows:

Constraint	Corresponding Extreme Points
2	(1) $X_{02} = 3$, $X_{11} = 7$, $X_{23} = 10$; (2) $X_{02} = 3$, $X_{11} = 8$, $X_{23} = 9$.
3	infeasible
4	(1) $X_{02} = 3$, $X_{11} = 8$, $X_{23} = 9$.
5	(1) $X_{02} = 3$, $X_{11} = 7$, $X_{23} = 10$; (2) $X_{02} = 3$, $X_{11} = 8$, $X_{23} = 9$.

Note that there is repetitions in the extreme points when different constraints are set at equality. Therefore, in the process of examination repetitive extreme points are omitted.

Appendix D

(i) Procedures for Forward and Backward Shifts:

This procedure is applied to one technology at a time and assumes the investment schedule for the other technologies is fixed.

Initialization: t = 1 and i = 0.

Step 1. Begin with period t and find an interval (t1,t2), $t \leq t1 < t2 \leq T$ such that $X_{it1} > 0$, $X_{it2} > 0$ and $X_{i\tau} = 0$ ($\tau = t$, t+1, ..., t1-1, t1+1, ..., t2-1.), set k = t1 and go to step 2. If no such interval can be found and i < N, set i = i+1; t =1 and go to step 1. If $i \geq N$, stop.

Step 2. k = k + 1. Let S denote the excess capacity in technology i based on demands up to period k, i.e., it is the maximal amount of investment in technology i which can be postponed to period k. If no such S can be found, go to Step 4. Otherwise, consider the following modifications:

$$X'_{it1} = X_{it1} - S,$$
$$X'_{ik} = X_{ik} + S + X_{it2}$$
$$X'_{it2} = 0$$

The incremental cost is as follows:
$$f_{it1}(X'_{it1}) + f_{ik}(X'_{ik}) - f_{it1}(X_{it1}) - f_{ik}(X_{ik}) - f_{it2}(X_{it2}).$$

If the incremental cost is negative, go to step 3. Otherwise, the solution is unchanged and go to step 4.

Step 3. Update the solution with the solution in Step 2 and the current objective value. Go to step 5.

Step 4. If k < t2, go to step 2. Otherwise, go to step 5.

Step 5. t = t2+1 and go to step 1.

The procedure of Backward Shift is similar to Forward Shift except that in Backward Shift we start with period T and proceed in reverse chronological order.

(ii) Procedures for Global Shifts:

This procedure is also applied to one technology at a time and assumes the investment schedule for the other technologies is fixed. Let C_{it} denote the cumulative capacity for technology i up to period t.

Initialization: i = 0.

Step 1: Compute the effective demand, $\overline{d}_{it}$ for technology i, t = 1, 2, ..., T. If i = 0, $\overline{d}_{it} = \sum\limits_{i=1}^{N} \max\{d_{it} - C_{it}, 0\}$. If i $\neq$ 0, $\overline{d}_{it} = \max$

$\{d_{it} - (C_{0t} - \sum\limits_{\substack{j=1 \\ j\neq i}}^{N} \max\{d_{jt} - C_{jt}, 0\}), 0\}$.

Note that $\sum\limits_{\substack{j=1 \\ j\neq i}}^{N} \max\{d_{jt} - C_{jt}, 0\}$ is the amount of flexible capacity

required in period t to satisfy demands for all products other than i. C_{0t} $- \sum\limits_{\substack{j=1 \\ j\neq i}}^{N} \max\{d_{jt} - C_{jt}, 0\}$ is the remaining flexible capacity which can be

used for demand i.

Step 2. Using $\overline{d}_{it}$ as the net demand i at period t, we find an optimal expansion policy for technology i by dynamic programming (A problem similar to this one is described in Section 4.1 for deriving lower bounds.).

Step 3. If the resulting solution is better than the current solution for technology i, update the solution and objective value. Otherwise, the solution is unchanged.

Step 4. If i < N, i = i + 1 and go to Step 1. Otherwise, stop.

(iii)   Procedures for technology Shift:

This procedure is applied to one period at a time.

$$\text{Let } \delta_{it} = \begin{cases} 1 & \text{if } X_{it} > 0 \\ 0 & \text{otherwise} \end{cases}.$$

Initialization: $t = 1$.

Step 1. If $\sum_{i=1}^{N} \delta_{it} \leq 1$, go to step 2. Otherwise, consider the following

modifications: $X'_{0t} = X_{0t} + \sum_{i=1}^{N} X_{it}$

The incremental cost is as follows:

$$f_{0t}(X'_{0t}) - f_{0t}(X_{0t}) - \sum_{i=1}^{N} f_{it}(X_{it})$$

If the incremental cost is negative, go to step 3. Otherwise, do not change the solution and go to Step 2.

Step 2. If $X_{0t} = 0$, go to step 4. Otherwise, perform the following procedure:

Initialization: $j = 0$

2(a): $j = j + 1$. Let S denote the maximal amount of flexible capacity that may be replaced by dedicated technology of type j without affecting feasibility. If $S = 0$, no modification is required and go to 2(b). Otherwise, consider the following modifications:

$$X'_{0t} = X_{0t} - S$$
$$X'_{jt} = X_{jt} + S$$

The incremental cost will be
$$f_{0t}(X'_{0t}) + f_{jt}(X'_{jt}) - f_{0t}(X_{0t}) - f_{jt}(X_{jt}).$$

If the incremental is negative, go to step 3. Otherwise, do not change the solution and go to 2(b).

2(b): If $j = N$, go to step 4. Otherwise, go to 2(a).

Step 3. Update the current solution and the objective value and go to step 4.

Step 4. If $t < T$, $t = t + 1$, go to step 1. Otherwise, stop.

(iv) Procedures for Interval Shift:

Initialization: $t = 1$.

Step 1. Begin with period t and find an interval $(t1, t2)$, $t \le t1 < t2 \le T$ such that $\sum_{i=1}^{2} X_{it1} > 0$, $\sum_{i=1}^{2} X_{it2} > 0$ and $X_{i\tau} = 0$ ($i = 1$ and 2; $\tau = t$, $t+1, ..., t1-1, t1+1, ..., t2-1.$). If no such interval can be found, stop.

Step 2: Without considering capacity additions in periods $t1$ and $t2$, find effective demand for each technology and effective demands for combinations of technologies as explained in **SP** in section 4.

Step 3. Solve a new **SP** based on the effective demands with the beginning period as $t1$ and the ending period as $t2$. If the optimal solution to this **SP** improves current solution, go to step 4. Otherwise, go to step 5.

Step 4. Update the current solution and objection value.

Step 5. $t = t2+1$. If $t < T$, go to step 1. Otherwise, stop.

Appendix E

Mixed Integer Programming Formulation:

Additional Notation:

$$Y_{it} = \begin{cases} 1 & \text{if } X_{it} > 0 \\ 0 & \text{otherwise} \end{cases} \qquad i = 0, 1, 2; t = 1, 2,..., T$$

F_{it}: fixed charge of investment in type i at period t, i = 0, 1, 2;
$\qquad$ t = 1, 2,..., T

C_{it}: variable cost of investment in type i at period t, i = 0, 1, 2;
$\qquad$ t = 1, 2,..., T

$$f_{it}(X_{it}) = \begin{cases} 0 & \text{if } X_{it} = 0 \\ F_{it}+C_{it}X_{it} & \text{if } X_{it} > 0 \end{cases}$$

M = constant that represents an upper bound in the capacity addition in any period. (For example, M is set at $\sum\limits_{i=1}^{2} \sum\limits_{t=1}^{T} d_{it}$ in the computational experiments.)

$$\text{Min:} \quad \sum_{i=1}^{2} \sum_{t=1}^{T} (F_{it} Y_{it} + C_{it} X_{it}) + \sum_{t=1}^{T} (F_{0t} Y_{0t} + C_{0t} X_{0t})$$

subject to:

$$\sum_{\tau=1}^{t} X_{i\tau} + \sum_{\tau=0}^{t} X_{0\tau} \geq d_{it} \qquad i = 1, 2; t = 1,..., T \qquad (1)$$

$$\sum_{i=1}^{2} \sum_{\tau=1}^{t} X_{i\tau} + \sum_{\tau=0}^{t} X_{0\tau} \geq \sum_{i=1}^{2} d_{it} \qquad t = 1, 2,..., T \qquad (2)$$

$$X_{it} - MY_{it} \leq 0 \qquad\qquad i = 0, 1, 2; t = 1, 2,..., T \qquad (3)$$

$$X_{it} \geq 0 \qquad\qquad i = 0, 1, 2; t = 1, 2,..., T \qquad (4)$$

$$Y_{it} \in \{0, 1\} \qquad\qquad i = 0, 1, 2; t = 1, 2,..., T \qquad (5)$$

Appendix F

Proof of Proposition 1 in Chapter 4:

To prove the proposition, it is sufficient to show that the coefficient matrix of the constraint set of CP is a totally unimodular matrix (TUM) (See Papadimitriou and Steiglitz (1982), p 316-18.). First, we add surplus and slack variables to inequalities of (3.1) and (3.2) to make them equality constraints. The corresponding coefficient matrix has the following form:

$$[\; A1 \;|\; A2 \;|\; A3 \;]$$

$$\text{where } A1 = \begin{bmatrix} L & & & & \\ & L & & & \\ & & \cdot & & \\ & & & L & \\ & & & & L \end{bmatrix}, \quad A2 = \begin{bmatrix} I & & & & \\ & I & & & \\ & & \cdot & & \\ & & & & I \\ -I & -I & \cdots & & -I \end{bmatrix}, \quad A3 = \begin{bmatrix} -I & & & & \\ & -I & & & \\ & & \cdot & & \\ & & & -I & \\ & & & & -I \end{bmatrix}$$

I is a $T \times T$ identity matrix and L is a $T \times T$ lower triangular matrix in which elements on and below the diagonal take a value of $+1$ and others are zero.

Note that submatrices A1 and A2 correspond to variables X_{it} and Y_{it}. Submatrix A3 represents surplus variables. It is well known that A2 is a TUM.

Claim 1: A1 is a TUM.

Since A1 is a block diagonal matrix, we only need to prove that L is a TUM. Take any k×k arbitrary submatrix in L. If there are two or more rows with same number of $+1$s or at least one row of zeros in L, the submatrix is a singular matrix. Otherwise, the matrix must have K rows each of which has a unique number of $+1$s. By rearranging the rows in the order of number of $+1$s, the matrix can be reduced to a lower triangular matrix with a determinant $+1$. Hence, A1 is a TUM.

Next we prove that [A1, A2] is a TUM. For this we only need to consider the submatrices of the following type:

$$\begin{bmatrix} B1 & 0 & C1 \\ B2 & 0 & 0 \\ 0 & B3 & C2 \end{bmatrix}$$

where B1, B2 and B3 are submatrices in A1 and C1 and C2 are submatrices in A2.

By virtue of the position of the null matrices in this array, we have the determinant of the above matrix equal to $|$ det B2 $| * |$ det B3 $| * |$ det C1 $| = \pm 1$ or 0. Therefore, [A1, A2] is a TUM.

Since A3 is an identity matrix, [A1, A2, A3] is also a TUM (see Papadimitriou and Steiglitz (1982), p316-318.) and the proposition follows.   Q. E. D.

Appendix G

Proposition: Suppose assumption (b) in Section 3 holds and product demands follow uniform distribution. Then, feasible solutions for the problem TPCT(X_0) form a convex set.

Proof:

Let $X^1 = (X_1{}^1, X_2{}^1)$ and $X^2 = (X_1{}^2, X_2{}^2)$ be two feasible solutions for TPCT(X_0). We prove the proposition by showing $X^0 = (X_1{}^0, X_2{}^0) = (\frac{1}{2} (X_1{}^1 + X_1{}^2), \frac{1}{2} (X_2{}^1 + X_2{}^2))$ is also feasible for TPCT(X_0).

Observe that Constraints (1') and (4) are linear in X_1 and X_2 for given X_0 and are trivially satisfied by X^0. Hence, to prove the proposition, it is sufficient to show that X^0 satisfies Constraint (2').

Since X^1 and X^2 are feasible, then

$$X_1{}^1 X_2{}^1 + X_0(X_1{}^1 + X_2{}^1) \geq S_{12}\, b_1\, b_2 - \frac{X_0{}^2}{2}$$

$$X_1{}^2 X_2{}^2 + X_0(X_1{}^2 + X_2{}^2) \geq S_{12}\, b_1\, b_2 - \frac{X_0{}^2}{2}$$

It follows that

$$X_1{}^1 X_2{}^1 + X_1{}^2 X_2{}^2 + X_0(X_1{}^1 + X_2{}^1) + X_0(X_1{}^2 + X_2{}^2)$$
$$\geq 2[S_{12}\, b_1\, b_2 - \frac{X_0{}^2}{2}] \quad \text{(a1)}$$

Without loss of generality, we assume that $X_1{}^1 \geq X_1{}^2$. To show that X^0 satisfies (2'), consider the following two cases:

Case 1: $\quad X_2{}^1 \geq X_2{}^2$

In this case $X_1{}^1 \geq X_1{}^0 \geq X_1{}^2$ and $X_2{}^1 \geq X_2{}^0 \geq X_2{}^2$. Hence, $X_1{}^1 X_2{}^1 \geq X_1{}^0 X_2{}^0 \geq X_1{}^2 X_2{}^2$, and Constraint (2') is trivially satisfied by X^0.

Case 2: $X_2^1 < X_2^2$

In this case, $X_1^0 + X_2^0 = \frac{1}{2}(X_1^1 + X_1^2 + X_2^1 + X_2^2)$. Further it is easy to show: $2 X_1^0 X_2^0 \geq X_1^1 X_2^1 + X_1^2 X_2^2$ (a2)

We omit the algebra since it is not particularly instructive. From (a1) and (a2) it follows that

$$X_1^0 X_2^0 + X_0(X_1^0 + X_2^0)$$
$$\geq \frac{1}{2}[X_1^1 X_2^1 + X_1^2 X_2^2 + X_0(X_1^1 + X_2^1) + X_0(X_1^2 + X_2^2)]$$
$$\geq S_{12}\, b_1\, b_2 - \frac{X_0^2}{2}$$

The proposition follows directly from the inequality above.

Appendix H

An Example for Finding an Optimal Solution for TPCT(X_0) :

Consider the subproblem with $X_0 = 10$ for Example 2 in Section 5. (See Table 1 for data.) The corresponding TPCT(X_0) may be formulated as follows:

$$[\text{TPCT}(10)]\ \ F(X_0 = 10) = \min \sum_{i=1}^{2} f_i(X_i)$$

$$\text{subject to:}$$
$$0.25X_2 + X_1 \geq 21.25$$
$$0.4X_1 + X_2 \geq 34$$
$$(X_1 + 10)(X_2 + 10) \geq 900$$
$$0 \leq X_1 \leq 25$$
$$0 \leq X_2 \leq 40$$

The feasible region corresponding for TPCT(10) is shown in the accompanying figure. Using the procedure described in Figure 3 we obtain the following:

P_1: $X_1 = 20$ and $X_2 = 20$. P_1 is not feasible.
P_2 : $X_1 = 14.17$ and $X_2 = 28.333$; the corresponding investment cost

$$(\sum_{i=1}^{2} (F_i + C_i X_i)) = 303.521$$

P_5: $X_1 = 11.25$ and $X_2 = 40$; the corresponding investment cost
    $= 364.75$
P_7: $X_1 = 25$ and $X_2 = 24$; the corresponding investment cost $= 349.00$
    P_2, P_5 and P_7 are all feasible with P_2 as the best solution and P_7
    as the second. Following Proposition 3, P_6, P_8, P_9 and P_{10}
    must be infeasible. P_3 and P_4 are calculated as follows:
P_3: $X_1 = 14.606$ and $X_2 = 26.577$; P_3 is infeasible.
P_4: $X_1 = 13.258$ and $X_2 = 28.697$; P_4 is infeasible.

Thus P_2 is the optimal solution to TPCT(10).

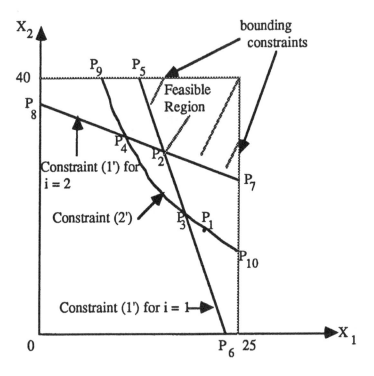

BIBLIOGRAPHY

Andreou, S.A., 1990, A Capital Budgeting Model for Product-Mix
    Flexibility, *J. Mfg. Oper. Mgt.* 63, 5-23.

Berliner, C. and Brimson, J.A. (eds.), 1988, Cost Management for
    Today's Advanced Manufacturing, *(Boston: Harvard Business
    School Press)*.

Bird, C.G. 1987, A Stochastic Programming with Resource Approach
    to Capacity Planning. Working paper General Motors, Warren,
    Michigan.

Boyd, D.W., R.L. Phillips and S.G. Regulinski, 1982, A Model of
    Technology Selection by Cost Minimizing Producers,
    Management Science, 24 (4), 418-424.

Burstein, M.C, 1986, Finding the Economical Mix of Rigid and
    Flexible Automation for Manufacturing Systems, Proceedings
    of the Second ORSA/TIMS Conference on Flexible
    Manufacturing systems: Operations Research Models and
    Applications, (Elsevier Publishers B.V., Amsterdam).

Butcher, W.S., Haimes, Y.Y. and Hall, W.A., 1969, Dynamic
    Programming for the Optimal Sequencing of Water Supply
    Projects, *Water Resources Research*, 5, 1196-1204.

Chakravarty, A.K., 1986, Decision Rules for Switching Flexible
    Capacity Between Competing Products, School of Business
    Administration, University of Wisconsin-Milwaukee.

139

-------, 1989, Analysis of Flexibility with Rationing for a Mix of Manufacturing Facilities, *The International Journal of Flexible Manufacturing Facilities*, 2, 43-61.

Cohen, M.A. and Halperin, R.M, 1986, Optimal Technology Choice in a Dynamic-Stochastic Environment, *Journal of Operations Management*, **6** (3), 317-331.
------ and Moon, S., 1989, The Impact of Production Scale Economics, Manufacturing Complexity and Transportation Costs on Supply Chain Facility Networks, Decision Science Working Paper.

Cooper, R. and Kaplan, R.S., 1988a, How Cost Accounting Systematically Distorts Product Costs, *Management Accounting*, April, 96-105.

------ and Kaplan, R.S., 1988b, Measure Costs Right: Make the Right Decisions, *Harvard Business Review*, Vol. 66, No. 5, 96-1-5.

Dempster, M.A.H., Fisher, M.L., Jensen, L., Lagcweg, B.J., Leustra, H.J., and Rinnooy Kan, A.H.G., 1981, Analytical Evaluations of Hierarchical Planning Systems, *Operations Research*, **9**, 707-716.

Erlenkotter, D, 1967, Two Producing Areas--Dynamic Programming Solutions, *Investments for Capacity Expansion: Size, Location and Time-Phasing*, pp. 210-227, (A.S. Manne (ed.). MIT Press, Cambridge, Mass.).

------ 1973a, Sequencing of Interdependent Hydroelectric Projects, *Water Resources Research*, **9**, 21-27.

------ 1973b, Sequencing Expansion Projects, *Operations Research*, **21**, 542-547.

------ 1974, Dynamic Programming Approach to Capacity Expansion with Specialization, *Management Science*, 21, 360-363.

------ 1975, Comments on "Optimal Timing Sequencing and Sizing of Multiple Reservoir Surface Water Supply Facilities" by L. Becker and W.W-G. Yeh, *Water Resources Research*, 11, 380-381.

------ 1976, Coordinating Scale and Sequencing Decisions for Water Resources Projects, *Economic Modeling for Water Policy Evaluation*, 97-112. (North-Holland/TIMS Studies in the Management Sciences. Vol. 3. North-Holland, Amsterdam, Holland).

------ 1977, Capacity Expansion with Imports and Inventories, *Management Science*, 23, 694-702.

------ 1989, The General Optimal Market Area Model, *Annals of Operations Research*, 18, 45-70.

Fine, C.H, 1989, Development in Manufacturing Technology and Economic Evaluation Models. Working Paper, #02139, Sloan School of Management, MIT.

------ and Freund, R.M., 1990, Optimal Investment in Product-Flexible Manufacturing Capacity, *Management Science*, 36 (4), 449-466.

Fong, C.O. and Rao, M.R., 1975, Capacity Expansion with Two Producing Regions and Concave Costs, *Management Science*, 22, 331-339.

------ and Srinivasan, V., 1981a, The Multi-region Dynamic Capacity Expansion Problem, Part I, *Operations Research*, 29, 787-799.

------ and Srinivasan, V., 1981b, The Multiregion Dynamic Capacity Expansion Problem, Part II, *Operations Research*, 29, 800-816.

------ and Srinivasan V., 1986, The Multi-region Dynamic Capacity Expansion Problem: An Improved Heuristic, *Management Science*, **32**, 1140-1152.

Freidenfelds, J., 1980, Capacity Expansion when Demand Is a Birth-Death Process, *Operations Research*, **28**, 712-721.

------ 1981, Near Optimal Solution of a Two-Type Capacity Expansion Problem, *Computers and Operations Research*, **8**, 221-239.

Gaimon, C, 1986, The Strategic Decision to Acquire Flexible Technology. Working Paper, The Ohio State University, Columbus, Ohio.

------ 1989, The Strategic Decision to Acquire Flexible Technology, *Operations Research*, **37**, 410- 425.

Gerwin, D, 1989, Manufacturing Flexibility in the CAM Era, *Business Horizon*, **37**, 410-425.

Goldhar, J.D. and Jelink, M., 1983, Plan for Economies of Scope, *Harvard Business Review*, November-December, 141-149.

------ and Jelink, M., 1985, Computer Integrated Flexible Manufacturing: Organizational, Economic and Strategic Implication, *Interface*, **15**(3), 94-105.

Gupta, D., Buzacott, J.A., and Gerchak, Y., 1988, Economic Analysis of Investment Decisions in Flexible Manufacturing Systems. Working Paper, Department of Management Science, University of Waterloo, Waterloo, Ontario, Canada.

------, Gerchak, D.Y. and Buzacott, J.A., 1990, The Optimal Mix of Flexible and Dedicated Manufacturing Capacitites: Hedging Against Demand Uncertaintly, Working Paper, McMaster University, Canada.

Hax, A.C. and Candea, D., 1984, *Production and Inventory Management*, Prentice Hall, Inc., Englewood, Ontario, 215-228.

------ and Meal, H.C., Hierarchical Integration of Production Planning and Scheduling, North Holland/TIMS, Studies in Management Sciences, Vol. 1, *Logistics*, North Holland, American Elsevier, 1975, 53-69.

Hinomoto, H, 1965, Capacity Expansion with Facilities under Technological Improvement, *Management Science*, **11**, 581-592.

Hung, H.K. and Rikkers, R.F., 1974, A Heuristic Algorithm for the Multi-Period Facility Location Problem. Paper presented at the 45th Joint National Meeting of ORSA/TIMS, Boston.

Hutchinson, G.K., and Holland, J.R., 1982, The Economic Value of Flexible Automation, *Journal of Manufacturing Systems*, **1**, 215-228.

Jacoby, H.D. and Loucks, D.P., 1972, Combined Use of Optimization and Simulation Models in River Basin Planning, *Water Resources Research*, **8**, 1401-1414.

Jaikumar, R, 1986, Post-industrial Manufacturing, *Harvard Business Review*, **64** (6), 69-76.

Jalinek, M. and Goldar, J. D., 1983, The Interface between Strategy and Manufacturing Technology, *Columbia Journal of World Business*, Spring, 26-35.

------ and Goldar, J.D., 1984, The Strategic Implications of the Factory of the Future, *Sloan Management Review*, Spring, 29-37.

Kalotay, A.J, 1973, Capacity Expansion and Specialization, *Management Science*, **20**, 56-64.

------ 1975, Joint Capacity Expansion without Rearrangement, *Operations Research Quarterly*, **26**, 649-658.

Kaplan, R.S, 1983, Measuring Manufacturing Performance: A New Challenge for Managerial Accounting, *The Accounting Review*, Vol. LVIII, No. 4, 686-705.

------ 1986, Must CIM be Justified by Faith Alone? *Harvard Business Review*, **64** (2), 87-95.

Karnani, A, 1983, The Trade-off Between Production and Transportation Costs in Determining Optimal Size, *Strategic Management Journal*, 4, 45-54.

Klincewicz, J.G. and Luss, H., 1985, Optimal Timing Decisions for the Introduction of New Technologies, *European Journal of Operations Research*, **20**, 211-220.

------ Luss, H. and Yu, C.S., 1988, A Large-scale Multilocation Capacity Planning Model, *European Journal of Operational Research*, **34**, 178-190.

Lee, S.B. and Luss, H., 1987, Multifacility-type Capacity Expansion Planning: Algorithms and Complexities, *Operations Research*, **35**, 249-253.

Lenstra, J.K., Rinnooy Kan, A.H.G. and Stougie, L., 1984, A Framework for the Probabilities Analysis of Hierarchical Planning Systems, *Annals of Operations Research*, **1**, 23-42.

Li, S. and Tirupati, D., 1992, Technology Choice and Capacity Expansion with Two Product Families: Tradeoffs between Scale and Scope., *International Journal of Production Research*, 30(A), 887-907.

------ and Tirupati, D., 1990b, Dynamic Capacity Expansion Problem with Multiple Products: Technology Selection and Timing of Capacity Additions., Opertions Research (forthcoming).

Lieberman, M.B., 1989, Capacity Utilization: Theoretical Models and Empirical Tests, *European Journal of Operations Research*, **40**, 155-168.

Lundin, R.A. and Morton, T.E., 1975, Planning Horizon for the Dynamic Lot Size Model: Zabel vs. Protective Procedures and computational Results, *Operations Research*, **23**(4), 711-734.

Luss, H, 1979, A capacity Expansion Model for Two Facility Types, *Naval Research Logistics Quarterly*, **26**, 291-303.

------ 1980, A Network Flow Approach for Capacity Expansion Problems with Two Facility Types, *Naval Research Logistics Quarterly*, **27**, 597-608.

------ 1982, Operations Research and Capacity Expansion Problems: A Survey, *Operations Research*, **30**, 907-947.

------ 1983, A Multi-facility Capacity Expansion Model with Joint Expansion Set-Up Costs, *Naval Research Logistics Quarterly*, **30**, 97-111.

------ 1986, A Heuristic for Capacity Planning with Multiple Facility Types, *Naval Research Logistics Quarterly.*, **33**, 686-701.

Manne, A.S, 1961, Capacity Expansion and Probabilistic Growth, *Econometrica*, **29**, 632-649.

------ (ed.), 1967, *Investments for Capacity Expansion: Size, Location and Time-phasing*, (MIT Press, Cambridge, Mass.).

------ and Veinott, A.F., Jr., 1967, Optimal Plant Size with Arbitrary Increasing Time Paths of Demand, *Investments for Capacity Expansion Size, Location and Time-Phasing*, pp. 198-190, (Manne (ed.) MIT Press, Cambridge, Mass.).

Meredith, J.R. and Suresh, N., 1986, Justification Techniques for Advanced Manufacturing Technologies, *International Journal of Production Research*, **24** (5), 1986.

Merhaut, J.M., 1975, A Dynamic Programming Approach to Joint Capacity Expansion without Rearrangement. Masters Thesis, Graduate School of Management, University of California at Los Angeles, Calif.

Meyer, A., Nakane, J., Miller, J.G. and K. Ferdows, 1989, Flexibility: The Next Competitive Battle the Manufacturing Futures Survey, *Strategic Management Journal*, **10**, 135-144.

Morin, T.L. and Esogbue, A.M.O., 1971, Some Efficient Dynamic Programming Algorithms for the Optimal Sequencing and Scheduling of Water-Supply Projects, *Water Resources Research*, **7**, 479-484.

Neebe, A.W. and Rao, M.R., 1983, The Discrete-time Sequencing Expansion, *Operations Research*, **31** (3), 546- 558.

Noori, H., 1987, Economics of Integration: A New Manufacturing Focus, Mimeograph, Research Center for Management of New Technology, Wilfred Laurier University, Waterloo, Ontario, Canada.

Papadimitriou, C.H. and Steiglitz, 1982, *Combinatorial Optimization: Algorithms and Complexity*, Prentice Hall Inc., Englewood Clifs, New Jersey.

Rao, R.C. and Rutenberg, D.P., 1977, Multilocation Plant Sizing and Timing, *Management Science*, **23**, 1187-1198.

Sethi, A. K, and Sethi, S.P., 990, Flexibility in Manufacturing: A Survey, *The International Journal of Flexible Manufacturing Systems*, **2**, 289-32.

Srinivasan, V., 1967, Geometric Rate of Growth of Demand, Investments for Capacity Expansion: Size, Location and Time-Phasing, (A.S. Manne (ed.). MIT Press, Cambridge, Mass.).

Swamidass, P.M., Manufacturing Flexibility, *Monograph*, **2**, Operations Management Association.

Tombak, M. and Meyer, A.D., 1988, Flexibility and FMS: An Empirical Analysis, *IEEE Transactions on Engineering Management*, **35** (2), 101-107.

Vander Veen, D.J. and Jordan, W.C., 1989, Analyzing Trade-offs Between Machine Investment and Utilization, *Management Science*, **35**, 1215-1226.

Vienott, Jr. A.F., 1967, Optimal Plant Size with Arbitrary Increasing Time Paths of Demand, Investments for Capacity Expansion: Size, Location and Time-Phasing, (A.S. Manne (ed.). MIT Press, Cambridge, Mass.).

Vietorisz, T. and Manne, A.S., 1963, Chemical Process, Plant Location, and Economics of Scale, *Studies in Process Analysis: Economy-Wide Production Capabilities*, 136-158, (A.S. Manne and H.M. Markowits (eds.) John Wiley, New York).

Wagner, H.M. and Whitin, T.M., 1958, Dynamic Version of the Economic Lot Size Model, *Management Science*, **5**, 89-96.

Whitt, W. and Luss, H., 1981, The Stationary Distribution of a Stochastic Clearing Process, *Operations Research*, **29**, 294-308.

Wilson, L.O., and Kalotay, A.J., 1976, Alternating Policies for Nonrearrangeable Networks, *INFOR*, **14**, 193-211.

Young, G.K., Moseley, J.C. and Evenson, D.E., 1970, Time Sequencing of Element Construction in a Multi-Reservoir System, *Water Resource Bulletin*, **9**, 528-541.

INDEX

A
Adding Constraint Method 71
all flexible technology strategy 99
allocation decisions 45
Availability Method 70

C
CAD 3, 7, 39, 79
CAE 79
CAM 3, 39, 79
CIM 3, 7, 37, 39, 40, 59, 79, 81
Cohen and Halperin's model
    stochastic demand 23-25
concave minimization 50, 83
convex set 86, 87
cost function
    concave 11, 53, 80, 82, 87, 97
    fixed-charge 73, 98, 99
    linear 98
    power 12, 73, 98, 99
cushion 100

D
demand
    deterministic 9
    dynamic 10
    stochastic 9
demand pattern 4
dependent demand 54
discrete uniform distribution 98
dual lower bound 70
dynamic and general demand 42

dynamic and uncertain demands 39
dynamic concave cost functions 62
dynamic product mixes 40

E
economic evaluation of flexibility 40
economies of scale 4, 7, 42, 60, 63, 64, 83, 85, 98
economies of scope 39, 40, 60, 80
embedded network structures 45
expansion strategies 47

F
FA 7, 59
Fine and Freund's model
        multi-products, stochastic demand 33-34
FMS 3, 7, 37, 39, 40, 59, 81
Fong and Srinivasan's model
        multi-region 18-19, 65
Forward or Backward Shift 51, 68

G
Global Shift 51, 68
Gupta et al.'s model
        two products with stochastic demand 28-30

H
Hinomoto's model
        technology improvement 20-22

I
Independent demand 54
inflexible technology strategy 99
Interval Shift 69
inventory 44, 79
Investment Model
        multi-product 62
        two product 62
        two product model 5

Investment model applications
    automobile, fabrication and discrete part manufactures 36
    communications industry 35
    process and chemical industries 34
    water resources 36
investment tradeoff 60

L
Lagrangian 71, 89
Li and Tirupati's model
    multi-product, deterministic demand 31-33
Look-Ahead Procedure 66
lower bound 52-53, 68, 69, 71
Luss' model
    two products with deterministic demand 26-28

M
machine investment and utilization decisions 62
Manne's model
    single product 14-15
manufacturing flexibility 39, 103
mix flexibility 4
model-based approach 60
multiple-product families 57

N
Neebe and Rao's model
    project investment 16-17
network flow problem 27
non-linear investment cost functions 57
normal distribution 87, 101

O
operating cost 76, 101
operating policies 88
operational flexibility 3
optimal mix of flexible and dedicated technologies 57
optimal mix of technology 101

P
Period Shift 69
planning horizon
    finite 12
    infinite 13
pre-allocation 104
product mix 7-9, 39, 81, 104
product mix flexibility 40, 62, 99

Q
quality improvement 79

R
rationing policies 84
rolling horizon 46, 66

S
seasonal demands 44
service level 4, 82, 83, 84, 86, 89, 93, 98
strategic investment planning model 43

T
technology
    dedicate 11
    dedicated 56
    flexible 10, 56
technology mix 79
Technology Shift 51, 69
Temporal and Technology Shift 52
Temporal Shift 51, 68
two-product families 42, 84
two-stage heuristic 65
two-stage stochastic program 42

U
uniform distribution 80, 87

Z
zero set-up cost 79

For Product Safety Concerns and Information please contact our EU
representative GPSR@taylorandfrancis.com Taylor & Francis Verlag GmbH,
Kaufingerstraße 24, 80331 München, Germany

Printed and bound by CPI Group (UK) Ltd, Croydon, CR0 4YY
08/05/2025
01864470-0002